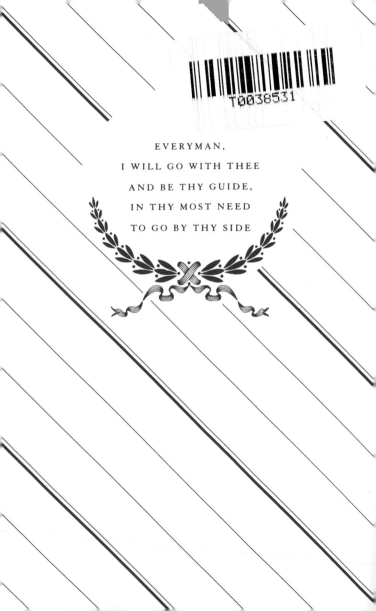

EVERYMAN,
I WILL GO WITH THEE
AND BE THY GUIDE,
IN THY MOST NEED
TO GO BY THY SIDE

EVERYMAN'S LIBRARY
POCKET POETS

RIVER POEMS

••••••••••••••••••

EDITED BY
HENRY HUGHES

EVERYMAN'S LIBRARY
POCKET POETS

Alfred A. Knopf New York London Toronto

THIS IS A BORZOI BOOK
PUBLISHED BY ALFRED A. KNOPF

This selection by Henry Hughes
first published in Everyman's Library, 2022
Copyright © 2022 by Everyman's Library
Engravings by Paul Gentry

A list of acknowledgments to copyright owners appears
at the back of this volume.

everymanslibrary.com
www.everymanslibrary.co.uk

ISBN 978-0-593-53553-0 (US)
978-1-84159-827-7 (UK)

Library of Congress Control Number: 2022938665

A CIP catalogue record for this book is available
from the British Library

Typography by Peter B. Willberg

Typeset in the UK by Input Data Services Ltd, Isle Abbotts,
Somerset

Printed and bound in Germany
by GGP Media GmbH, Pössneck

CONTENTS

Foreword 13

HEADWATERS

Hymn to the Nile 23

Ezekiel 47:9 25

LAOZI *From* Dao De Jin 26

WANG WEI Cormorant Bank 27

        From Gold Dust Spring 27

HORACE *From* Odes, III 28

DAFYDD LLWYD OF MATHAFARN *From* To the
    River Dyfi 29

ALEXANDER POPE *From* Windsor-Forest 30

SAMUEL TAYLOR COLERIDGE To the River
    Otter 32

GEORGE GORDON, LORD BYRON First Fountain 33

TRADITIONAL ENGLISH SONG The Waters
    of Tyne 34

TRADITIONAL AMERICAN SONG Oh, Shenandoah 35

RALPH WALDO EMERSON The River 36

HENRY DAVID THOREAU *From* The Journal . . 38

CARL SANDBURG Languages 39

PABLO NERUDA Amazon 40

TED HUGHES River 41

VASKO POPA Great Lord Danube 42

GABRIEL OKARA The Call of the River Nun . . 43

JIM HARRISON River III 45

DAVID WAGONER Talking to Barr Creek 46

DUANE NIATUM Evening Near the Hoko
    River   48

CHARLES WRIGHT Cloud River   50

WILL BURNS Bridges of the Wendover Arm ..   51

JANE CLARKE Against the Flow   52

RAPIDS & POOLS

WANG WEI Luan Family Rapids   55

HENRY VAUGHAN The Water-Fall   56

GEORGE GORDON, LORD BYRON Could Love ..   58

NIKOLAUS LENAU Look into the Stream   59

EDGAR ALLAN POE To the River   60

ALFRED, LORD TENNYSON *From* The Brook ..   61

ROBERT LOUIS STEVENSON Looking-Glass
    River   63

THOMAS HARDY The Something that
    Saved Him   64

GERARD MANLEY HOPKINS Inversnaid   66

WILLIAM BUTLER YEATS Stream and Sun
    at Glendalough   67

IVAN BUNIN With the Current.   68

ROBERT FROST Too Anxious for Rivers   69

WILLIAM CARLOS WILLIAMS River Rhyme. . ..   70

ANNE RIDLER River God's Song   71

TED HUGHES Low Water   73

DIANE WAKOSKI The Canoer   74

KAY RYAN The Niagara River   75

GARY SNYDER The Canyon Wren   76

DON McKAY Pool   78

SEAMUS HEANEY Perch 79

GEFFREY DAVIS Upriver, Downstream 80

JOHN BURNSIDE Heatwave 81

DONOVAN DARLING Haskin's Creek, August,
    As Revival 83

TRINITY HERR Topography 85

NATASHA TRETHEWEY Elegy 86

RAYMOND CARVER Simple 88

FREEZE, FLOW & FLOOD

FUJIWARA NO SADAYORI Winter Dawn,
    Uji River 91

EDMUND SPENSER *From* Prothalamion 92

JOHN DRYDEN London After the
    Great Fire, 1666 94

HENRY WADSWORTH LONGFELLOW *From*
    To the River Charles 95

WALT WHITMAN *From* Crossing Brooklyn
    Ferry 96

SIDNEY LANIER The Song of the
    Chattahoochee 99

RUDYARD KIPLING The River's Tale 101

THOMAS HARDY Overlooking the River Stour . . 103

KENJI MIYAZAWA Along that Frozen
    Little River 104

WILLIAM BUTLER YEATS Down by the
    Salley Gardens 105

T. S. ELIOT *From* The Dry Salvages 106

W. H. AUDEN River Profile 107

A. R. AMMONS River 110

JAMES WRIGHT To Flood Stage Again. 112

WILLIAM STAFFORD Ask Me 113

HAYDEN CARRUTH The Water 114

DON MCKAY Night Skating on the
    Little Paddle River 115

SHUNTARŌ TANIKAWA *From* River 116

WENDELL BERRY The River Voyagers 117

LOUISE GLÜCK Early December in
    Croton-on-Hudson 118

LOUISE ERDRICH I Was Sleeping Where the
    Black Oaks Move 119

OWEN SHEERS Liable to Floods 121

KAREN HOULE Pleasure Craft 123

PAUL MULDOON Clonfeacle. 124

ALICE OSWALD Birdwatcher 125

EMILY ROSKO Flood Plain 127

GILLIAN CLARKE Glacier 129

TROUBLED WATERS

From The Epic of Gilgamesh 133

ROBERT HERRICK Dean-Bourn, A Rude
    River in Devon 134

WILLIAM BLAKE Why Should I Care for the
    Men of Thames 135

TRADITIONAL AFRICAN-AMERICAN SPIRITUAL
    Roll, Jordan, Roll 136

TRADITIONAL AFRICAN-AMERICAN SPIRITUAL
    Deep River 137

WALT WHITMAN Cavalry Crossing a Ford 138

JÓNAS HALLGRÍMSSON The Sog, Iceland 139

WILFRED OWEN Shadwell Stair 140

LOUIS MACNEICE Charon . . . . . : 141

RABINDRANATH TAGORE The Golden Boat . . 142

PAUL DRESSER On the Banks of the Wabash,
     Far Away 144

H. D. Leda 145

WILLIAM CARLOS WILLIAMS *From* Paterson . . 147

OSCAR HAMMERSTEIN II *From* Ol' Man River . . 149

CONSTANCE URDANG The River 150

STEVIE SMITH The River God 151

TED HUGHES Ophelia 153

U. A. FANTHORPE Rising Damp 154

CITTADHAR HṚDAYA River 156

WILLIAM MEREDITH At the Confluence of the
     Colorado and the Little Colorado 158

CHARLES BUKOWSKI The Rivers 160

TSITSI ELLA JAJI Limpopo Blues 162

JORGE HUMBERTO CHÁVEZ The River 163

TRACY K. SMITH Wade in the Water 164

KIT EVANS Riverbed Blues 166

MEDITATIONS & MEANDERINGS

LAOZI *From* Dao De Jin 169

DU FU Thoughts on Traveling By Night 170

KOBAYASHI ISSA Cricket Singing 171

UEJIMA ONITSURA Below the Jumping
     Sweetfish 171

WILLIAM WORDSWORTH Upon Westminster
    Bridge 172
OSCAR WILDE Symphony in Yellow 173
MARCEL PROUST The Carafes of the
    Vivonne 174
GUILLAUME APOLLINAIRE Mirabeau Bridge . . 175
WALLACE STEVENS The River of Rivers
    in Connecticut 177
LANGSTON HUGHES The Negro Speaks
    of Rivers 178
BUDDHADĀSA BHIKKHU The River Bends
    but the Water Does Not 179
PAULINE STAINER Pouring the Sand Mandala
    into the Thames 180
SYLVIA PLATH Faun 181
KATHLEEN RAINE By the River Eden 182
ROBERT BLY Driving Toward the
    Lac Qui Parle River 185
JOHN BETJEMAN Henley-on-Thames 186
GRACE PALEY Suddenly There's Poughkeepsie 188
JAMES REANEY To the Avon River,
    Above Stratford, Canada 190
GARY SNYDER River in the Valley 192
EAVAN BOLAND Anna Liffey 194
MARY OLIVER At Black River 203
SAM HAMILL A Snapshot of Susitna 205
PAUL MULDOON The Waking Father 206
ALICE OSWALD *From* Dart 207
TCHICAYA U TAM'SI Brush Fire 208

TODD DAVIS Gnosis 209
PAULA BOHINCE La Seine 210

DELTAS

ZHANG RUOXU Moonlight on the Spring River 215
MATSUO BASHO Mogami River 216
          Hot Summer Day 216
EMILY DICKINSON My River Runs to Thee .. 217
          Least Rivers 217
WILLIAM GIBSON *From* The River Columbia .. 218
ALICE MEYNELL The Visiting Sea 220
VALERY BRYUSOV To Myself 221
HART CRANE Repose of Rivers.. 222
JOHN MASEFIELD *From* The River 223
MARINA TSVETAEVA *From* The Notebook,
    No. 8 225
ROBINSON JEFFERS Salmon-Fishing 226
RUTH PITTER The Estuary 227
EUGENIO MONTALE Delta 229
JUDITH WRIGHT Northern River 230
THEODORE ROETHKE River Incident 232
SHUNTARŌ TANIKAWA River 233
JAMES DICKEY Awaiting the Swimmer 234
RAYMOND CARVER Where Water Comes
    Together with Other Water 236
DAVID BOTTOMS In a Jon Boat During a
    Florida Dawn 238
RICHARD LAMBERT River 240
ROBIN ROBERTSON Tillydrone Motte 241

11

JOHN SIBLEY WILLIAMS Sediment 243

PHILIP GROSS Sluice Angel 244

BRUCE BOND The Delta 246

SCOTT STARBUCK The Hunger. 248

Acknowledgments 249

FOREWORD

It was our first river trip together, falling in love and maybe afraid of falling as we slid the wooden drift boat down the icy ramp into Oregon's Siletz River, running cold and clear through the dripping dark vault of basalt and towering evergreens. Chloë pointed out gray dipper birds walking underwater, acrobatic otters, and rolling Chinook salmon; and I rowed, avoiding mossy rocks and overhanging snags, reading the gravelly bends and blue chutes. We talked and gazed, anchoring in a turquoise pool under a golden stand of alder to cast our flies. "This feels like a poem," Chloë said.

Her observation reflects an ancient confluence of water and words. Rivers were the arteries of our first civilizations – the Tigris and Euphrates of Mesopotamia, India's Ganges, Egypt's Nile, the Yellow River of China – and have nourished modern cities from London to New York, so it's natural that poets have for centuries drawn essential meanings and metaphors from their endless currents. Rivers teem with symbolic significance: they have long been ritual sites for funerals and baptisms, for deaths and rebirths; they slake our thirst, nourish our crops, and provide us with food, transportation, and power.

This collection of poems honors the geographic and cultural legacies of rivers, "Loving them all the way back to their source," as Raymond Carver vows.

"Hymn to the Nile," from the second millennium BCE, hails the life-giving Egyptian river: "If the Nile smiles the earth is joyous." Fifteen hundred years later, the Old Testament prophet, Ezekiel, reminds us that "wherever the river goes, every living creature that swarms will live." Concurrently in China, the *Dao De Jin* affirms that "The highest good is like water, / Nourishing all things." Water settles in low places, coming "close to the Dao," the *way*, the natural order of the universe. East Asian reverence for rivers surfaces in Chinese Tang dynasty poets and Japanese haiku masters such as Matsuo Basho and his transformative Mogami River that "Has poured the hot summer sun / Into the ocean."

In the West, Edmund Spenser sets a flowery and swan-filled wedding on the "Sweet Thames," asking it to "run softly, till I end my song." England's River Thames runs through many poems in this collection, hailed by John Dryden as the quenching salvation after the Great Fire of 1666, and by Alexander Pope as the "Father of the British Floods." Modern portraits of the Thames by Wilfred Owen, Louis MacNeice, and Stevie Smith recognize the watershed's industrial degradation and urban squalor; but the river is nonetheless imbued with mysterious powers. "They say I am a foolish old smelly river," Stevie Smith writes. "But they do not know of my wide original bed / Where the lady waits, with her golden sleepy head."

Ted Hughes and Alice Oswald speak the river voices

of western England; John Burnside takes us for a cool swim on a hot summer night in Scotland; and Welsh poet Owen Sheers gauges human arrogance in the face of flooding. In "Clonfeacle," Paul Muldoon tells the riverside story of St. Patrick as a parable of negotiation amid the sectarian conflicts in Northern Ireland, and the struggles and stamina of Irish womanhood are brilliantly personified in Eavan Boland's "Anna Liffey."

Across the Atlantic, American voices spring from their own deep pools of memory. Louise Erdrich witnesses a devastating flood on Minnesota's Chippewa reservation. Seeing the distressed herons flying above, her grandfather tells her "These are the ghosts of the tree people" and the poet longs to "dream our way back" to those sacred origins. Struggle and hope echo through the African-American spirituals "Roll, Jordan, Roll" and "Deep River," and are honored afresh in Tracy K. Smith's "Wade in the Water": "Singing that old blood-deep song / That dragged us to those banks." Walt Whitman's expansive "Crossing Brooklyn Ferry" achieves an urban transcendence beyond place and time. Our collective connection to rivers is powerfully realized in Langston Hughes' sonorous evocation of identity, "The Negro Speaks of Rivers," where he contemplates the Mississippi transformed by emancipation and the currents that enlarge our consciousness: "My soul has grown deep like the rivers."

Flowing or still, water reflects the cycle of life.

Canadian poet Don McKay recalls ice skating on the Little Paddle River where "Some may glimpse a lost one / in the spaces between the skaters or the watchers." On Florida's Black River, Mary Oliver watches a napping alligator, fearing its predatory ferocity and reminded that "death comes before / the rolling away / of the stone." And in a moving elegy, Natasha Trethewey relives salmon fishing with her beloved late father.

Rivers don't stop at political or social boundaries, as Mexican poet Jorge Humberto Chávez dramatizes in his troubling portrait of the Rio Grande. Chilean Nobel laureate Pablo Neruda offers a sensual tribute to his beloved multinational Amazon River; Tchicaya U Tam'si marks the confluence of his life with that of the complicated Congo; and Serbian poet Vasko Popa hails the "great Lord Danube" as it glimmers across Europe. The poetry in this collection flows from over twenty nations in millions of miles of changing currents.

Since our first river adventure in Oregon, Chloë and I have explored the Columbia, Amazon, Hudson, Thames, Elbe, Hvítá, Seine, and countless smaller waterways, like the Cherwell near her family's home in Oxfordshire where we endeavored to punt away a summer afternoon, admiring swans, drinking wine, and reading poetry. Whether it was the wine, a stuck pole, or some rough meter that caused my unexpected swim, we were soon revived by laughter and cups of Pimm's at the Boat House. Whatever trouble we get into, boating in sticky canals or tricky rapids, in high and low water, fair weather or foul, the rivers and their flow of words endure, deepening and carrying us on.

HENRY HUGHES

RIVER POEMS

HEADWATERS

A river watering the garden flowed from Eden.

GENESIS, 2:10

They shall have gardens beneath which rivers flow, and therein all that they wish.

QUR'AN, SURAH AN-NAHL, 6:30

HYMN TO THE NILE

     Adoration to the Nile!
      Hail to thee, O Nile!
   Who manifestest thyself over this land,
   Who cometh to give life to Egypt!
Mysterious is thy issuing forth from the darkness,
On this day whereon it is celebrated!
     Watering the orchards created by Ra
     To cause all the cattle to live
Thou givest the earth to drink, O inexhaustible one!
     Loving the fruits of Seb
     And the first fruits of Nepera
Thou causest the workshops of Ptah to prosper.

     Lord of the fish, during the inundation,
     No bird alights on the crops!
Thou createst corn, thou bringest forth the barley,
Assuring perpetuity to the temples.
If thou ceasest thy toil and thy work,
Then all that exists is in anguish.
If the gods suffer in heaven,
Then the faces of men waste away . . . .

If the Nile smiles the earth is joyous,
Every stomach is full of rejoicing,
Every spine is happy,
Every jawbone crushes its food . . . .
A festal song is raised for thee on the harp,

O Nile, come and prosper!
O thou who makest men to live through his flocks,
Likewise his flocks through his orchards,
　　Come and prosper, come,
　　O Nile, come and prosper!

And wherever the river goes, every living creature that swarms will live, and there will be very many fish. For this water goes there, that the waters of the sea may become fresh; so everything will live where the river goes.

From DAO DE JIN

The highest good is like water,
Nourishing all things and not contending with them,
Settling in loathsome places and thus coming close to
    the Dao.

Chapt. VIII

The river and sea can be kings of a hundred valleys
Because they lie below them.

Therefore, the sage who desires to rule over the people
must first humble himself, speaking to them
    from below.
To lead the people, one must follow behind them.

Therefore, when this ruler stands above people,
They are not oppressed.
When he leads the people,
They are not endangered.
The world will exalt him
And not grow weary of his rule.

Because he does not contend for power,
No one under heaven can contend with him.

Chapt. LXVI

LAOZI (*fl.* 550 BCE)
26   TRANS. JIN LEI

CORMORANT BANK

Suddenly dipping among red lotus flowers,
It emerges from bulrushes and quivers.
Standing alone, wet and disheveled,
With a fish in its beak, atop an old log.

From GOLD DUST SPRING

Drink each day from Gold Dust Spring
And you should live a thousand years.

WANG WEI (699–761)
TRANS. JIN LEI

From ODES, III

XIII

Brighter than any bauble made out of glass,
you deserve, Bandusian spring, our thanks in wine,
    flowers, and even a young kid,
        just beginning to grow his horns.

That would have prepared him for love and
        doing battle –
except that we shall sacrifice him to you
    and your cool waters will stream
        with his warm, bright red blood.

The hottest days of summer cannot affect you,
for even then you provide delightful relief
    for any tired and thirsty plowmen
        and woolly sheep of the wandering flock.

I shall make you one of the famous springs
praising you and the holm oak above you
    at the mouth of the rocky cave from which
        your welcome waters come babbling forth.

HORACE (65−8 BCE)
TRANS. DAVID R. SLAVITT

From TO THE RIVER DYFI

Fair-browed Dyfi of Arthur's lover spawned,
A goddess, a bright companion,
Strong and young, yet older
Than belief in Jesus you are;
A capricious maid in the bosom of winter,
A slender girl in summer.
'Tis God who pours you, Dyfi,
From the mountain into the briny.
Gentle Father Tydecho transformed
Your waters to milk from end to end.
Neither woods nor meadow will deter thee,
A great serpent flowing to a ruby-red sea.

DAFYDD LLWYD OF MATHAFARN (1420–*c*.1500)
TRANS. SIÂN SAUNDERS and MARTIN DAVIS

From WINDSOR-FOREST

The silver Stream her Virgin Coldness keeps,
For ever murmurs, and for ever weeps;
Still bears the Name the hapless Virgin bore,
And bathes the Forest where she rang'd before.
In her chast Current oft the Goddess laves,
And with Celestial Tears augments the Waves.
Oft in her Glass the musing Shepherd spies
The headlong Mountains and the downward Skies,
The watry Landskip of the pendant Woods,
And absent Trees that tremble in the Floods;
In the clear azure Gleam the Flocks are seen,
And floating Forests paint the Waves with Green.
Thro' the fair Scene rowl slow the lingring Streams,
Then foaming pour along, and rush into the *Thames*.

  Thou too, great Father of the *British* Floods!
With joyful Pride survey'st our lofty Woods,
Where tow'ring Oaks their growing Honours rear,
And future Navies on thy Shores appear.
Not *Neptune*'s self from all his Streams receives
A wealthier Tribute, than to thine he gives.
No Seas so rich, so gay no Banks appear,
No Lake so gentle, and no Spring so clear.
Nor *Po* so swells the fabling Poet's Lays,
While led along the Skies his Current strays,
As thine, which visits *Windsor*'s fam'd Abodes,
To grace the Mansion of our earthly Gods.
Nor all his Stars above a Lustre show,

Like the bright Beauties on thy Banks below;
Where *Jove*, subdu'd by mortal Passion still,
Might change *Olympus* for a nobler Hill.

TO THE RIVER OTTER

Dear native Brook! wild Streamlet of the West!
   How many various-fated years have passed,
   What happy and what mournful hours, since last
I skimmed the smooth thin stone along thy breast,
   Numbering its light leaps! Yet so deep imprest
Sink the sweet scenes of childhood, that mine eyes
I never shut amid the sunny ray, –
   But straight with all their tints thy waters rise,
Thy crossing plank, thy marge with willows grey, –
   And bedded sand that, veined with various dyes,
Gleamed through thy bright transparence!
      On my way,
   Visions of Childhood! oft have ye beguiled
Lone manhood's cares, yet waking fondest sighs:
   Ah! that once more I were a careless child.

FIRST FOUNTAIN

Could I remount the river of my years
To the first fountain of our smiles and tears,
I would not trace again the stream of hours
Between their outworn banks of withered flowers,
But bid it flow as now – until it glides
Into the number of the nameless tides.

THE WATERS OF TYNE

I cannot get to my love, if I would dee,
The water of Tyne runs between him and me;
And here I must stand with a tear in my eye,
Both sighing and sickly my sweetheart to see.

O where is the boatman? my bonny hinny!
O where is the boatman? bring him to me –
To ferry me over the Tyne to my honey,
And I will remember the boatman and thee.

O bring me a boatman, I'll give any money,
And you for your trouble rewarded shall be –
To ferry me over the Tyne to my honey,
Or scull him across that rough river to me.

OH, SHENANDOAH

Oh, Shenandoah, I long to hear you,
Away, you rolling river
Oh, Shenandoah, I long to hear you
Away, I'm bound away, cross the wide Missouri.

Oh, Shenandoah, I love your daughter,
Away, you rolling river
Oh, Shenandoah, I love your daughter
Away, I'm bound away, cross the wide Missouri.

Oh, Shenandoah, I'm bound to leave you,
Away, you rolling river
Oh, Shenandoah, I'm bound to leave you
Away, I'm bound away, cross the wide Missouri.

Oh, Shenandoah, I long to see you,
Away, you rolling river
Oh, Shenandoah, I long to see you
Away, I'm bound away, cross the wide Missouri.

TRADITIONAL AMERICAN SONG

THE RIVER

And I behold once more
My old familiar haunts; here the blue river,
The same blue wonder that my infant eye
Admired, sage doubting whence the traveler came, –
Whence brought his sunny bubbles ere he washed
The fragrant flag-roots in my father's fields,
And where thereafter in the world he went.
Look, here he is, unaltered, save that now
He hath broke his banks and flooded all the vales
With his redundant waves.
Here is the rock where, yet a simple child,
I caught with bended pin my earliest fish,
Much triumphing, – and these the fields
Over whose flowers I chased the butterfly,
A blooming hunter of a fairy fine.
And hark! where overhead the ancient crows
Hold their sour conversation in the sky: –
These are the same, but I am not the same,
But wiser than I was, and wise enough
Not to regret the changes, tho' they cost
Me many a sigh. Oh, call not Nature dumb;
These trees and stones are audible to me,
These idle flowers, that tremble in the wind,
I understand their faery syllables,
And all their sad significance. The wind,
That rustles down the well-known forest road –
It hath a sound more eloquent than speech.

The stream, the trees, the grass, the sighing wind,
All of them utter sounds of 'monishment
And grave parental love.
They are not of our race, they seem to say,
And yet have knowledge of our moral race,
And somewhat of majestic sympathy,
Something of pity for the puny clay,
That holds and boasts the immeasurable mind.
I feel as I were welcome to these trees
After long months of weary wandering,
Acknowledged by their hospitable boughs;
They know me as their son, for side by side,
They were coeval with my ancestors,
Adorned with them my country's primitive times,
And soon may give my dust their funeral shade.

From THE JOURNAL

For the first time it occurred to me this afternoon what a piece of wonder a river is – a huge volume of matter ceaselessly rolling through the fields and meadows of this substantial earth, making haste from the high places, by stable dwellings of men and Egyptian Pyramids, to its restless reservoir. One would think that, by a very natural impulse, the dwellers upon the headwaters of the Mississippi and Amazon would follow in the trail of their waters to see the end of the matter.

– September 5, 1838

LANGUAGES

There are no handles upon a language
Whereby men take hold of it
And mark it with signs for its remembrance.
It is a river, this language,
Once in a thousand years
Breaking a new course
Changing its way to the ocean.
It is mountain effluvia
Moving to valleys
And from nation to nation
Crossing borders and mixing.
Languages die like rivers.
Words wrapped round your tongue today
And broken to shape of thought
Between your teeth and lips speaking
Now and today
Shall be faded hieroglyphics
Ten thousand years from now.
Sing – and singing – remember
Your song dies and changes
And is not here to-morrow
Any more than the wind
Blowing ten thousand years ago.

CARL SANDBURG (1878–1967)

AMAZON

Capital of the water's syllables,
patriarch father, you are
the secret eternity
of fecundations,
rivers like birds fall into you, you are covered by
the fire colored pistils
the great dead logs populate you with perfume
the moon can neither watch nor measure you.
You are loaded with green sperm
like a bridal tree, you are silvered
by the wild spring,
you are blushed wood,
blue between the moon of stones
dressed in ferruginous steam
slow as a planet's path

PABLO NERUDA (1904–73)
40   TRANS. JAIME MARROQUÍN ARREDONDO

RIVER

Fallen from heaven, lies across
The lap of his mother, broken by world.

But water will go on
Issuing from heaven

In dumbness uttering spirit brightness
Through its broken mouth.

Scattered in a million pieces and buried
Its dry tombs will split, at a sign in the sky,

At a rending of veils.
It will rise, in a time after times,

After swallowing death and the pit
It will return stainless

For the delivery of this world.
So the river is a god

Knee-deep among reeds, watching men,
Or hung by the heels down the door of a dam

It is a god, and inviolable.
Immortal. And will wash itself of all deaths.

TED HUGHES (1930–98)   41

GREAT LORD DANUBE

O great Lord Danube
In your veins flows
The blood of the white town

If you love it get up a moment
From your bed of love

Ride on your biggest carp
Pierce the leaden clouds
And visit your heavenly birthplace

Bring a gift to the white town
Fruits and birds and flowers of paradise

Bring too the stone which can be eaten
And a little air
Of which men do not die

The bell-towers will bow down to you
And the streets prostrate themselves before you
O great Lord Danube

VASKO POPA (1922–91)
TRANS. ANNE PENNINGTON and FRANCIS R. JONES

THE CALL OF THE RIVER NUN

I hear your call!
I hear it far away;
I hear it break the circle
of these crouching hills.

I want to view your face
again and feel your cold
embrace; or at your brim
to set myself and
inhale your breath; or
Like the trees, to watch
my mirrored self unfold
and span my days with
song from the lips of dawn.

I hear your lapping call!
I hear it coming through;
invoking the ghost of a child
listening, where river birds hail
your silver-surfaced flow.

My river's calling too!
Its ceaseless flow impels
my found'ring canoe down
its inevitable course.
And each dying year
brings near the sea-bird call,

the final call that
stills the crested waves
and breaks in two the curtain
of silence of my upturned canoe.

O incomprehensible God!
Shall my pilot be
my inborn stars to that
final call to Thee
O my river's complex course?

RIVER III

Saw a poem float by just beneath
the surface, another corpse of the spirit
we weren't available to retrieve.
It isn't comforting to admit that our days
are fatal, that the corpse of the spirit
gradually becomes the water and waits
for another, or perhaps you, to return
to where you belong, not in the acting
of a shaker sprinkling its salt
everywhere. You have to hold your old
heart lightly as the female river holds
the clouds and trees, its fish
and the moon, so lightly but firmly
enough so that nothing gets away.

TALKING TO BARR CREEK

Under the peachleaf willows, alders, and choke
    cherries,
By coltsfoot, devil's club, sweet-after-death,
And bittersweet nightshade,
Like a fool, I sit here talking to you, begging a favor,
A lesson as hard and long as your bed of stones
To hold me together.
At first, thinking of you, my mind slid down like
    a leaf
From source to mouth, as if you were only one
Piece of yourself at a time,
As if you were nowhere but here or there,
    nothing but now,
One place, one measure. But you are all at once,
Beginning through ending.
What man could look at you all day and not be
    a beggar?
How could he take his eyes at their face-value?
How could his body
Bear its dead weight? Grant me your endless,
    ungrudging impulse
Forward, the lavishness of your light movements,
Your constant inconstancy,
Your leaping and shallowing, your stretches of black
    and amber,
Bluing and whitening, your long-drawn wearing
    away.

Your sudden stillness.
From the mountain lake ten miles uphill to the
    broad river,
Teach me your spirit, going yet staying, being
Born, vanishing, enduring.

DAVID WAGONER (1926–2021)

EVENING NEAR THE HOKO RIVER

On the bank of this Klallam river, I am
at rest and fall to earth the way
birch leaves grow small and thin in music.
Like coast wind echoes from the sea,
faces of autumn emerge in orange
and gold and mauve. Crickets spring
moss-lined goodbyes on path,
sandbar and raccoon tracks.
Bear grass trampled down all summer
outshines the illegible animal ancestors
passing through the contrary mirrors of stars.

Yellow tulips claim there is no other world
than this hill which is as active
as the memory of a lavender field
in another country of the imagination's,
especially the one I saw in the eye
of a snail, rainbow's daughter. The cold
dampness of twigs and cones frames
the creatures of metamorphosis,
not the song higher than the osprey gliding
from one current to another above the river.
Desire rises and falls in the air
like the swallows chasing insects into fireweed,
reverses direction and zips through
the canyon, home to seed and wing.

The moon in a violet fancy dance,
vagabond in any season, any mood and light,
flings souvenirs to the dream catchers
running for the river, swings a cape
over shoulders as she goes to sleep
in the monolithic hollows of the sea.
The white horses of this beauty
take a step or two or three,
become the river's hoof beats of the mountain;
from the ruby-throated sky a sparrow
drops from branch to branch
into the heart-line of larch.

DUANE NIATUM (b. 1938)

CLOUD RIVER

The unborn children are rowing out to the far edge
    of the sky,
Looking for warm beds to appear in. How lucky they
    are, dressed
In their lake-colored gowns, the oars in their
    oily locks
Taking them stroke by stroke to circumference
    and artery . . .

I'd like to be with them still, pulling my weight,
Blisters like small white hearts in the waxed palms of
    my hands.
I'd like to remember my old name, and keep
    the watch,
Waiting for something immense and unspeakable to
    uncover its face.

BRIDGES OF THE WENDOVER ARM

Low-rise heat over the morning woods.
River-crisp reflections of sky and hillside.
A last brood of coots and in the big field to the east,
    skylarks.
Breeding behaviour well into October.
Everything a little too warm-blooded.
Pop of tennis balls and bees, still,
on the rosemary flowers and Himalayan honeysuckle
outside the bankside house we've long coveted.
Rooftops of the town through a gap in the trees
the light barely there – crow-light for the jackdaws
    to roost by.
Plans and happenstance. Nobody near.
Spooked birds in military contrail –
some doubt in all that I can see, all I can hear.

AGAINST THE FLOW

One day you knew you must turn,
begin to swim against the current,

leave the estuary waters, brackish
with sediment, head upstream

through riffles and deeps,
millraces that churn in spate,

over sheets of granite, across weirs,
into rapids that thunder-pound,

squeeze between boulders,
to the upper reaches of the river,

those waters of blanket-bog brown,
where you'd find a place in gravel and silt

to hollow a dip,
to spawn a life of your own.

RAPIDS & POOLS

Say, you are in the country; in some high land of lakes. Take almost any path you please, and ten to one it carries you down in a dale, and leaves you there by a pool in the stream. There is magic in it.

HERMAN MELVILLE
Moby-Dick

The river has come back to fit between its banks. To stick your hands into the river is to feel the cords that bind the earth together in one piece.

BARRY LOPEZ
River Notes

LUAN FAMILY RAPIDS

Gusts of wind in the autumn rain
Water rushing wild over stones
Leaping waves splash each other
A white egret is startled up,
Then settles down again

WANG WEI (699–761)
TRANS. JIN LEI

THE WATER-FALL

With what deep murmurs through time's silent
    stealth
Doth thy transparent, cool, and wat'ry wealth
Here flowing fall,
And chide, and call,
As if his liquid, loose retinue stay'd
Ling'ring, and were of this steep place afraid;
The common pass
Where, clear as glass,
All must descend
Not to an end,
But quicken'd by this deep and rocky grave,
Rise to a longer course more bright and brave.

Dear stream! dear bank, where often I
Have sate and pleas'd my pensive eye,
Why, since each drop of thy quick store
Runs thither whence it flow'd before,
Should poor souls fear a shade or night,
Who came, sure, from a sea of light?
Or since those drops are all sent back
So sure to thee, that none doth lack,
Why should frail flesh doubt any more
That what God takes, he'll not restore?

O useful element and clear!
My sacred wash and cleanser here,
My first consigner unto those
Fountains of life where the Lamb goes!
What sublime truths and wholesome themes
Lodge in thy mystical deep streams!
Such as dull man can never find
Unless that Spirit lead his mind
Which first upon thy face did move,
And hatch'd all with his quick'ning love.
As this loud brook's incessant fall
In streaming rings restagnates all,
Which reach by course the bank, and then
Are no more seen, just so pass men.
O my invisible estate,
My glorious liberty, still late!
Thou art the channel my soul seeks,
Not this with cataracts and creeks.

COULD LOVE

Could Love for ever
Run like a river,
And Time's endeavour
   Be tried in vain –
No other pleasure
With this could measure;
And like a treasure
   We'd hug the chain.
But since our sighing
Ends not in dying,
And, formed for flying,
   Love plumes his wing;
Then for this reason
Let's love a season;
But let that season be only Spring.

LOOK INTO THE STREAM

If you see your fortune pass you by
And not a thing remains,
A stream's a good place to cast your eye
Where everything waxes and wanes.

Oh! Within, within, just stop and gaze,
And you'll find it easier to miss
What's been torn from your heart's embrace –
Be it your truest bliss.

Look down into the river steadily
Until your tears can fall,
And through their warm rush see
The surging flood becoming small.

Dreaming becomes forgetfulness
The heart's wounds begin to close;
The soul sees with all its woe,
Itself reflected in the flow.

NIKOLAUS LENAU (1802–50)
TRANS. ANNA MUENCHRATH

TO THE RIVER

Fair river! in thy bright, clear flow
   Of crystal, wandering water,
Thou art an emblem of the glow
     Of beauty – the unhidden heart –
     The playful maziness of art
In old Alberto's daughter;

But when within thy wave she looks –
     Which glistens then, and trembles –
Why, then, the prettiest of brooks
     Her worshipper resembles;
For in my heart, as in thy stream,
   Her image deeply lies –
His heart which trembles at the beam
   Of her soul-searching eyes.

From THE BROOK
The Song of the Brook

I come from haunts of coot and hern,
    I make a sudden sally,
And sparkle out among the fern,
    To bicker down a valley.

By thirty hills I hurry down,
    Or slip between the ridges,
By twenty thorps, a little town,
    And half a hundred bridges.

Till last by Philip's farm I flow
    To join the brimming river,
For men may come and men may go,
    But I go on for ever.

I chatter over stony ways,
    In little sharps and trebles,
I bubble into eddying bays,
    I babble on the pebbles.

With many a curve my banks I fret
    By many a field and fallow,
And many a fairy foreland set
    With willow-weed and mallow.

I chatter, chatter, as I flow
   To join the brimming river,
For men may come and men may go,
   But I go on for ever.

I wind about, and in and out,
   With here a blossom sailing,
And here and there a lusty trout,
   And here and there a grayling,

And here and there a foamy flake
   Upon me, as I travel . . . .

LOOKING-GLASS RIVER

Smooth it slides upon its travel,
    Here a wimple, there a gleam –
        O the clean gravel!
        O the smooth stream!

Sailing blossoms, silver fishes,
    Paven pools as clear as air –
        How a child wishes
        To live down there!

We can see our coloured faces
    Floating on the shaken pool
        Down in cool places,
        Dim and very cool;

Till a wind or water wrinkle,
    Dipping martin, plumping trout,
        Spreads in a twinkle
        And blots all out.

See the rings pursue each other;
    All below grows black as night,
        Just as if mother
        Had blown out the light!

Patience, children, just a minute –
    See the spreading circles die;
        The stream and all in it
        Will clear by-and-by.

ROBERT LOUIS STEVENSON (1850–94)   63

THE SOMETHING THAT SAVED HIM

It was when
Whirls of thick waters laved me
Again and again,
That something arose and saved me;
Yea, it was then.

In that day
Unseeing the azure went I
On my way,
And to white winter bent I,
Knowing no May.

Reft of renown,
Under the night clouds beating
Up and down,
In my needfulness greeting
Cit and clown.

Long there had been
Much of a murky colour
In the scene,
Dull prospects meeting duller;
Nought between.

Last, there loomed
A closing-in blind alley,
        Though there boomed
A feeble summons to rally
        Where it gloomed.

        The clock rang;
The hour brought a hand to deliver;
        I upsprang,
And looked back at den, ditch and river,
        And sang.

INVERSNAID

This darksome burn, horseback brown,
His rollrock highroad roaring down,
In coop and in comb the fleece of his foam
Flutes and low to the lake falls home.

A windpuff-bonnet of fáwn-fróth
Turns and twindles over the broth
Of a pool so pitchblack, féll-frówning,
It rounds and rounds Despair to drowning.

Degged with dew, dappled with dew
Are the groins of the braes that the brook treads
        through,
Wiry heathpacks, flitches of fern,
And the beadbonny ash that sits over the burn.

What would the world be, once bereft
Of wet and of wildness? Let them be left,
O let them be left, wildness and wet;
Long live the weeds and the wilderness yet.

STREAM AND SUN AT GLENDALOUGH

Through intricate motions ran
Stream and gliding sun
And all my heart seemed gay:
Some stupid thing that I had done
Made my attention stray.

Repentance keeps my heart impure;
But what am I that dare
Fancy that I can
Better conduct myself or have more
Sense than a common man?

What motion of the sun or stream
Or eyelid shot the gleam
That pierced my body through?
What made me live like these that seem
Self-born, born anew?

WILLIAM BUTLER YEATS (1865–1939)

WITH THE CURRENT

"Young girl, what did you draw
With your umbrella in the luminous river?"
The girl opened her umbrella
And stretched out in her canoe.

"She loves me – she loves me not . . ." But the heart
Asks for love, like a flower.
Quietly, the current carries away
The umbrella and the white canoe.

IVAN BUNIN (1870–1953)
TRANS. A. MOLOTKOV

TOO ANXIOUS FOR RIVERS

Look down the long valley and there stands a
    mountain
That someone has said is the end of the world.
Then what of this river that having arisen
Must find where to pour itself into and empty?
I never saw so much swift water run cloudless.
Oh, I have been often too anxious for rivers
To leave it to them to get out of their valleys.
The truth is the river flows into the canyon
Of Ceasing-to-Question-What-Doesn't-Concern-Us,
As sooner or later we have to cease somewhere.
No place to get lost like too far in the distance.
It may be a mercy the dark closes round us
So broodingly soon in every direction.
The world as we know is an elephant's howdah;
The elephant stands on the back of a turtle;
The turtle in turn on a rock in the ocean.
And how much longer a story has science
Before she must put out the light on the children
And tell them the rest of the story is dreaming?
"You children may dream it and tell it tomorrow."

RIVER RHYME

The rumpled river
takes its course
lashed by rain

This is that now
that tortures
skeletons of weeds

and muddy waters
eat their
banks the drain

of swamps a bulk
that writhes and fat-
tens as it speeds.

RIVER GOD'S SONG

My eyes are white stones
That shine through water
As the moon shines
Through a glistening mist,
My limbs the supple ripples
That part like a fan
Or fuse into one,
Wrinkle and fade

Look for long,
It will disappear.

My name is Evenlode,
Windrush, or Dove;
Or else Alpheus,
Ladon, Leucyanias:
Water as dark
As a night with glittering
Stars of the frogbit;
Water so clear
That the peering fish
Fear their own shadows;
As sleek as oil,
As lines erased
On a carbon pad.
The racing weed
Is my green hair.

Stare in the pool –
My wraith is there
In a wreath of water
Around a rock;

Or boiling down
In white cascades
And braids of glass.
Choose my name
And paint my scene
After your choice,
I am still the river.
You passers by
Who share my journey,
You move and change,
I move and am the same;
You move and are gone,
I move and remain.

LOW WATER

                              This evening
The river is a beautiful idle woman.

The day's August burn-out has distilled
A heady sundowner.
She lies back. She is tipsy and bored.

She lolls on her deep couch. And a long thigh
Lifts from the flash of her silks.

Adoring trees, kneeling, ogreish eunuchs
Comb out her spread hair, massage her fingers.

She stretches – and an ecstasy tightens
Over her skin, and deep in her gold body

Thrills spasm and dissolve. She drowses.

Her half-dreams lift out of her, light-minded
Love-pact suicides. Copulation and death.

She stirs her love-potion – ooze of balsam
Thickened with fish-mucus and algae.

You stand under leaves, your feet in shallows.
She eyes you steadily from the beginning of the world.

THE CANOER

the hush of
the river
at 4 a.m.,
fish flipper their bellies across moss,
trees walk down to the very shoreline
thinking nobody is watching them,
his paddle darts in and out of
the water, getting better acquainted
each time with its own slippery
texture,
hands boggle out of the river
offering foam money in the corner of his eye.

In my own mind
I change the texture of the river,
super-imposing on it
a buffalo, bleeding in the hindquarters,
not raging but calm and taking
the waters. The river dries up
around him, and the skeleton of the buffalo
walks down the dried-out bed of an old river.

THE NIAGARA RIVER

As though
the river were
a floor, we position
our table and chairs
upon it, eat, and
have conversation.
As it moves along,
we notice – as
calmly as though
dining room paintings
were being replaced –
the changing scenes
along the shore. We
do know, we do
know this is the
Niagara River, but
it is hard to remember
what that means.

KAY RYAN (b. 1945)   75

THE CANYON WREN
for James and Carol Katz

I look up at the cliffs
But we're swept on by   downriver
                              the rafts
Wobble and slide over roils of water
      boulders shimmer
      under the arching stream
Rock walls straight up on both sides.
A hawk cuts across that narrow sky
                 hit by sun,

We paddle forward, backstroke, turn,
Spinning through eddies and waves
Stairsteps of churning whitewater.
      above the roar
      hear the song of a Canyon Wren.

A smooth stretch, drifting and resting.
Hear it again, delicate downward song

      ti ti   ti ti tee tee tee

Descending through ancient beds.
A single female mallard flies upstream –

Shooting the Hundred-Pace Rapids
Su Shih saw, for a moment,
        it all stand still
"I stare at the water:
        it moves with unspeakable slowness"

Dōgen, writing at midnight,

        "mountains flow

        "water is the palace of the dragon
        "it does not flow away.

We beach up at China Camp
Between piles of stone
Stacked there by black-haired miners,
        cook in the dark
        sleep all night long by the stream.

These songs that are here and gone,
Here and gone,
To purify our ears.

POOL

Early deepshadowed pool we come
on tip-toe to your whispers of fish, to flick
these flies, sol-fa,

                          touching
exactly on your surface.

The real flies hang
ardent in air
full of their own small destinies
vivid with undelivered news –

but wait:
let us enter with ritual
flexings of elbow and shoulder, let us know your
delicate contingency as virgins vaguely
deeply stirred would know

that somewhere in their sleep
the sleek trout lurk.

PERCH

Perch on their water-perch hung in the clear
    Bann River
Near the clay bank in alder-dapple and waver,

Perch we called "grunts", little flood-slubs, runty
    and ready,
I saw and I see in the river's glorified body

That is passable through, but they're bluntly holding
    the pass,
Under the water-roof, over the bottom, adoze,

Guzzling the current, against it, all muscle and slur
In the finland of perch, the fenland of alder, on air

That is water, on carpets of Bann stream, on hold
In the everything flows and steady go of the world.

UPRIVER, DOWNSTREAM
– for J

I read the water, and the edges
of the water, august poplars

casting shadows along the bank. Insect
hatches sometimes bloom

straight from the riffles – all of it
a wayward map to the trout

flexing just beneath the long arch
of my fly-line querying the current.

Alone, I rifle streamers through pockets
deep enough to hold fish large

as memory. With others, I will wade
waist-deep all day, for the small

paradise of watching someone
run their fingers along the belly

of what was once impossible
to touch. And release everything back.

HEATWAVE

After it rained, the back roads gusted with steam,
and the gardens along our street filled with the scent
of stocks and nicotiana,
but it didn't get properly hot till the night drew in,
humid and heavy as glass
on our well-kept lawn.
It was high in the summer. With everyone else
in town for the Lammas fair
I took the meadow-path to where the river
stalled on a sudden blackness: alders
shrouded in night and warmth, and the first slow owl
charting the further bank.

There was always movement there
beneath the slick of moonlight on the turning
water, like a life beneath the life
I understood as cattle tracks and birds:
a darker presence, rising from the stream,
to match my every move, my every breath.
Eel-black and cold, it melded in my flesh
with all the nooks and crannies of the world
where spawn appears, or changelings slip their skins
to ripen at the damp edge of the day,
still blurred with mud
and unrecovered song.

But that night, as the sky above me turned,
I found a different swimmer in the steady
shimmer of the tide,
a living creature, come from the other side
to slip into the cool
black water. I remember how she looked,
beneath the moon, so motiveless and white,
her body like a pod that had been shelled
and emptied: Mrs Pearce, my younger sister's
science teacher, turning in the lit
amazement of a joy that I could almost
smell, across the haze of drifting heat.

I was crouched beneath a stand
of willows and I guess she didn't see
the boy who watched her swim for half an hour
then turn for home beneath the August moon,
a half-smile on her face, her auburn hair
straggling and damp;
yet later, as I walked the usual streets,
I thought that she would stop and recognise
a fellow soul, with river in his eyes,
slipping home under a wave of light and noise,
and finding the key to her nights
in his soft, webbed fingers.

HASKIN'S CREEK, AUGUST, AS REVIVAL

We turn sun
bleached August

creekdamp
shadow alder

subterrain tea
ribboning foothills

ten thousand heartbeats

  We've been at this sixteen years

blanket lays
hips foaming

where two bodies meet

lapping
at the bends

  The funny thing about failure
  is the redemptive quality of its beauty

a bruised farmhouse

meadows burnt
ochre

swaying
by the old road

miracle creek

chill
when day glows

Do you remember
when we cozied up

all those summers ago?

And now she
stands before us

miraculous

curious crawfish
newts blackberry

fingertips
which float

moor mine
delicately

which hold
my daughter

so dearly

TOPOGRAPHY

pluck crawfish from craters
with naked fingers, tango
bare legged through nettle groves, welt
in the strange topography of ripening, reroute
familiar planes from mirror to map
the way a river does
with each revolutionary swelling, surging
into cramped beds, cut
through what we thought was rock.

TRINITY HERR (b. 1990)

ELEGY
For my father

I think by now the river must be thick
    with salmon. Late August, I imagine it

as it was that morning: drizzle needling
    the surface, mist at the banks like a net

settling around us – everything damp
    and shining. That morning, awkward

and heavy in our hip waders, we stalked
    into the current and found our places –

you upstream a few yards and out
    far deeper. You must remember how

the river seeped in over your boots
    and you grew heavier with that defeat.

All day I kept turning to watch you, how
    first you mimed our guide's casting

then cast your invisible line, slicing the sky
    between us; and later, rod in hand, how

you tried – again and again – to find
    that perfect arc, flight of an insect

skimming the river's surface. Perhaps
    you recall I cast my line and reeled in

two small trout we could not keep.
    Because I had to release them, I confess,

I thought about the past – working
    the hooks loose, the fish writhing

in my hands, each one slipping away
    before I could let go. I can tell you now

that I tried to take it all in, record it
    for an elegy I'd write – one day –

when the time came. Your daughter,
    I was that ruthless. What does it matter

if I tell you I *learned* to be? You kept casting
    your line, and when it did not come back

empty, it was tangled with mine. Some nights,
    dreaming, I step again into the small boat

that carried us out and watch the bank receding –
    my back to where I know we are headed.

SIMPLE

A break in the clouds. The blue
outline of the mountains.
Dark yellow of the fields.
Black river. What am I doing here,
lonely and filled with remorse?

I go on casually eating from the bowl
of raspberries. If I were dead,
I remind myself, I wouldn't
be eating them. It's not so simple.
It is that simple.

FREEZE, FLOW
& FLOOD

You know, they straightened out the Mississippi River in places, to make room for houses and livable acreage. Occasionally the river floods these places. "Floods" is the word they use, but in fact it is not flooding; it is remembering. Remembering where it used to be. All water has a perfect memory and is forever trying to get back to where it was. Writers are like that . . . I remember where I was before I was "straightened out."

TONI MORRISON
The Site of Memory

WINTER DAWN, UJI RIVER

Winter dawn, Uji River,
Fog thins and fades,
Revealing in shallows
The stakes of fishing nets

FUJIWARA NO SADAYORI (995–1045)
TRANS. NAOKO ISHIKURA SMITH

From PROTHALAMION

Calm was the day, and through the trembling air
Sweet breathing Zephyrus did softly play,
A gentle spirit, that lightly did delay
Hot Titan's beams, which then did glister fair;
When I whose sullen care,
Through discontent of my long fruitless stay
In prince's court, and expectation vain
Of idle hopes, which still do fly away
Like empty shadows, did afflict my brain,
Walked forth to ease my pain
Along the shore of silver streaming Thames,
Whose rutty bank, the which his river hems,
Was painted all with variable flowers,
And all the meads adorned with dainty gems,
Fit to deck maidens' bowers,
And crown their paramours,
Against the bridal day, which is not long:
   Sweet Thames, run softly, till I end my song.

There, in a meadow, by the river's side,
A flock of nymphs I chanced to espy,
All lovely daughters of the flood thereby,
With goodly greenish locks, all loose untied,
As each had been a bride;
And each one had a little wicker basket,
Made of fine twigs, entrailed curiously,
In which they gathered flowers to fill their flasket,

And with fine fingers cropt full featously
The tender stalks on high.
Of every sort, which in that meadow grew,
They gathered some; the violet pallid blue,
The little daisy, that at evening closes,
The virgin lily, and the primrose true,
With store of vermeil roses,
To deck their bridegrooms' posies
Against the bridal day, which was not long:
    Sweet Thames, run softly, till I end my song.

LONDON AFTER THE GREAT FIRE, 1666

Before, she like some shepherdess did show
   Who sate to bathe her by a river's side,
Not answering to her fame, but rude and low,
   Nor taught the beauteous arts of modern pride.

Now like a maiden queen she will behold
   From her high turrets hourly suitors come;
The East with incense and the West with gold
   Will stand like suppliants to receive her doom.

The silver Thames, her own domestic flood,
   Shall bear her vessels like a sweeping train,
And often wind, as of his mistress proud,
   With longing eyes to meet her face again.

The wealthy Tagus and the wealthier Rhine
   The glory of their towns no more shall boast,
And Seine, that would with Belgian rivers join,
   Shall find her lustre stained and traffic lost.

The venturous merchant who designed more far
   And touches on our hospitable shore,
Charmed with the splendour of this northern star
   Shall here unlade him and depart no more.

From TO THE RIVER CHARLES

River! that in silence windest
   Through the meadows, bright and free,
Till at length thy rest thou findest
   In the bosom of the sea!

Four long years of mingled feeling,
   Half in rest, and half in strife,
I have seen thy waters stealing
   Onward, like the stream of life.

Thou hast taught me, Silent River!
   Many a lesson, deep and long;
Thou hast been a generous giver;
   I can give thee but a song.

From CROSSING BROOKLYN FERRY

Flow on, river! flow with the flood-tide, and ebb with
    the ebb-tide!
Frolic on, crested and scallop-edg'd waves!
Gorgeous clouds of the sunset! drench with your
    splendor me, or the men and women generations
    after me!
Cross from shore to shore, countless crowds of
    passengers!
Stand up, tall masts of Mannahatta! stand up,
    beautiful hills of Brooklyn!
Throb, baffled and curious brain! throw out questions
    and answers!
Suspend here and everywhere, eternal float of
    solution!
Gaze, loving and thirsting eyes, in the house or
    street or public assembly!
Sound out, voices of young men! loudly and musically
    call me by my nighest name!
Live, old life! play the part that looks back on the
    actor or actress!
Play the old role, the role that is great or small
    according as one makes it!
Consider, you who peruse me, whether I may not in
    unknown ways be looking upon you;
Be firm, rail over the river, to support those who lean
    idly, yet haste with the hasting current;

Fly on, sea-birds! fly sideways, or wheel in large
    circles high in the air;
Receive the summer sky, you water, and faithfully
        hold it till all downcast eyes have time to take it
        from you!
Diverge, fine spokes of light, from the shape of my
        head, or any one's head, in the sunlit water!
Come on, ships from the lower bay! pass up or down,
        white-sail'd schooners, sloops, lighters!
Flaunt away, flags of all nations! be duly lower'd at
        sunset!
Burn high your fires, foundry chimneys! cast black
        shadows at nightfall! cast red and yellow light
        over the tops of the houses!
Appearances, now or henceforth, indicate what
        you are,
You necessary film, continue to envelop the soul,
About my body for me, and your body for you, be
        hung our divinest aromas,
Thrive, cities – bring your freight, bring your shows,
        ample and sufficient rivers,
Expand, being than which none else is perhaps more
        spiritual,
Keep your places, objects than which none else is
        more lasting.

You have waited, you always wait, you dumb,
     beautiful ministers,
We receive you with free sense at last, and are
     insatiate henceforward,
Not you any more shall be able to foil us, or withhold
     yourselves from us,
We use you, and do not cast you aside – we plant you
     permanently within us,
We fathom you not – we love you – there is perfection
     in you also,
You furnish your parts toward eternity,
Great or small, you furnish your parts toward
     the soul.

THE SONG OF THE CHATTAHOOCHEE

Out of the hills of Habersham,
Down the valleys of Hall,
I hurry amain to reach the plain,
Run the rapid and leap the fall,
Split at the rock and together again,
Accept my bed, or narrow or wide,
And flee from folly on every side
With a lover's pain to attain the plain
Far from the hills of Habersham,
Far from the valleys of Hall.

All down the hills of Habersham,
All through the valleys of Hall,
The rushes cried "Abide, abide,"
The willful waterweeds held me thrall,
The laving laurel turned my tide,
The ferns and the fondling grass said "Stay,"
The dewberry dipped for to work delay,
And the little reeds sighed "Abide, abide,
Here in the hills of Habersham,
Here in the valleys of Hall."

High o'er the hills of Habersham,
Veiling the valleys of Hall,
The hickory told me manifold
Fair tales of shade, the poplar tall
Wrought me her shadowy self to hold,

The chestnut, the oak, the walnut, the pine,
Overleaning, with flickering meaning and sign,
Said, "Pass not, so cold, these manifold
Deep shades of the hills of Habersham,
These glades in the valleys of Hall."

And oft in the hills of Habersham,
And oft in the valleys of Hall,
The white quartz shone, and the smooth brook-stone
Did bar me of passage with friendly brawl,
And many a luminous jewel lone
– Crystals clear or a-cloud with mist,
Ruby, garnet and amethyst –
Made lures with the lights of streaming stone
In the clefts of the hills of Habersham,
In the beds of the valleys of Hall.

But oh, not the hills of Habersham,
And oh, not the valleys of Hall
Avail: I am fain for to water the plain.
Downward the voices of Duty call –
Downward, to toil and be mixed with the main,
The dry fields burn, and the mills are to turn,
And a myriad flowers mortally yearn,
And the lordly main from beyond the plain
Calls o'er the hills of Habersham,
Calls through the valleys of Hall.

THE RIVER'S TALE

Twenty bridges from Tower to Kew —
(Twenty bridges or twenty-two) —
Wanted to know what the River knew,
For they were young and the Thames was old.
And this is the tale that the River told: —

"I walk my beat before London Town,
Five hours up and seven down.
Up I go till I end my run
At Tide-end-town, which is Teddington.
Down I come with the mud in my hands
And plaster it over the Maplin Sands.
But I'd have you know that these waters of mine
Were once a branch of the River Rhine,
When hundreds of miles to the East I went
And England was joined to the Continent.

I remember the bat-winged lizard-birds,
The Age of Ice and the mammoth herds,
And the giant tigers that stalked them down
Through Regent's Park into Camden Town.
And I remember like yesterday
The earliest Cockney who came my way,
When he pushed through the forest that lined
        the Strand
With paint on his face and a club in his hand.
He was death to feather and fin and fur.

He trapped my beavers at Westminster.
He netted my salmon, he hunted my deer,
He killed my heron off Lambeth Pier.
He fought his neighbour with axes and swords,
Flint or bronze, at my upper fords,
While down at Greenwich, for slaves and tin,
The tall Phoenician ships stole in,
And North Sea war-boats, painted and gay,
Flashed like dragon-flies, Erith way;
And Norseman and Negro and Gaul and Greek
Drank with the Britons in Barking Creek,
And life was gay, and the world was new,
And I was a mile across at Kew!
But the Roman came with a heavy hand,
And bridged and roaded and ruled the land,
And the Roman left and the Danes blew in –
And that's where your history-books begin!"

OVERLOOKING THE RIVER STOUR

The swallows flew in the curves of an eight
     Above the river-gleam
     In the wet June's last beam:
Like little crossbows animate
The swallows flew in the curves of an eight
     Above the river-gleam.

Planing up shavings of crystal spray
     A moor-hen darted out
     From the bank thereabout,
And through the stream-shine ripped his way;
Planing up shavings of crystal spray
     A moor-hen darted out.

Closed were the kingcups; and the mead
     Dripped in monotonous green,
     Though the day's morning sheen
Had shown it golden and honeybee'd;
Closed were the kingcups; and the mead
     Dripped in monotonous green.

And never I turned my head, alack,
     While these things met my gaze
     Through the pane's drop-drenched glaze,
To see the more behind my back. . . .
O never I turned, but let, alack,
     These less things hold my gaze!

THOMAS HARDY (1840–1928)

ALONG THAT FROZEN LITTLE RIVER

Along that frozen little river
Many small dark terraces
Behind the day
Up to the sharp, treeless lava neck
Cold, cold-looking, continued on and on

KENJI MIYAZAWA (1896–1933)
TRANS. NAOKO ISHIKURA SMITH

DOWN BY THE SALLEY GARDENS

Down by the salley gardens my love and I did meet;
She passed the salley gardens with little
    snow-white feet.
She bid me take love easy, as the leaves grow on
    the tree;
But I, being young and foolish, with her would
    not agree.

In a field by the river my love and I did stand,
And on my leaning shoulder she laid her snow-white
    hand.
She bid me take life easy, as the grass grows on
    the weirs;
But I was young and foolish, and now am full
    of tears.

From THE DRY SALVAGES

I do not know much about gods; but I think that
    the river
Is a strong brown god – sullen, untamed and
    intractable,
Patient to some degree, at first recognised as a
    frontier;
Useful, untrustworthy, as a conveyor of commerce;
Then only a problem confronting the builder of
    bridges.
The problem once solved, the brown god is almost
    forgotten
By the dwellers in cities – ever, however, implacable,
Keeping his seasons and rages, destroyer, reminder
Of what men choose to forget. Unhonoured,
    unpropitiated
By worshippers of the machine, but waiting, watching
    and waiting.
His rhythm was present in the nursery bedroom,
In the rank ailanthus of the April dooryard,
In the smell of grapes on the autumn table,
And the evening circle in the winter gaslight.

RIVER PROFILE

Our body is a moulded river
NOVALIS

Out of a bellicose fore-time, thundering
head-on collisions of cloud and rock in an
up-thrust, crevasse-and-avalanche, troll country,
deadly to breathers,

it whelms into our picture below the melt-line,
where tarns lie frore under frowning cirques,
    goat-bell,
wind-breaker, fishing-rod, miner's-lamp country,
already at ease with

the mien and gestures that become its kindness,
in streams, still anonymous, still jumpable,
flows as it should through any declining country
in probing spirals.

Soon of a size to be named and the cause of
dirty in-fighting among rival agencies,
down a steep stair, penstock-and-turbine country,
it plunges ram-stam,

to foam through a wriggling gorge incised in softer
strata, hemmed between crags that nauntle heaven,
robber-baron, tow-rope, portage-way country,
nightmare of merchants.

Disembogueing from foothills, now in hushed
          meanders,
now in riffling braids, it vaunts across a senile
plain, well-entered, chateau-and-cider-press country,
its regal progress

gallanted for a while by quibbling poplars,
then by chimneys: led off to cool and launder
retort, steam-hammer, gasometer country,
it changes colour.

Polluted, bridged by girders, banked by concrete,
now it bisects a polyglot metropolis,
ticker-tape, taxi, brothel, foot-lights country,
a la mode always.

Broadening or burrowing to the moon's phases,
turbid with pulverized wastemantle, on through
flatter, duller, hotter, cotton-gin country
it scours, approaching

the tidal mark where it puts off majesty,
disintegrates, and through swamps of a delta,
punting-pole, fowling-piece, oyster-tongs country,
wearies to its final

act of surrender, effacement, atonement
in a huge amorphous aggregate no cuddled
attractive child ever dreams of, non-country,
image of death as

a spherical dew-drop of life. Unlovely
monsters, our tales believe, can be translated
too, even as water, the selfless mother
of all especials.

RIVER

I shall
   go down
      to the deep river, to the moonwaters,
where the silver
willows are and the bay blossoms,

to the songs
   of dark birds,
      to the great wooded silence
of flowing
forever down the dark river

silvered at the moon-singing of hidden birds:

27 March

the forsythia is out,
   sprawling like
yellow amoebae, the long
   uneven branches – pseudo-
podia –
   angling on the bottom
of air's spring-clear pool:

shall I
   go down
      to the deep river, to the moonwaters,
where the silver
willows are and the bay blossoms,

to the songs
   of dark birds,
      to the great wooded silence
of flowing
forever down the dark river

silvered at the moon-singing of hidden birds.

TO FLOOD STAGE AGAIN

In Fargo, North Dakota, a man
Warned me the river might rise
To flood stage again.
On the bridge, a girl hurries past me, alone,
Unhappy face.
Will she pause in wet grass somewhere?
Behind my eyes she stands tiptoe, yearning for
      confused sparrows
To fetch a bit of string and dried wheatbeard
To line her outstretched hand.
I open my eyes and gaze down
At the dark water.

ASK ME

Some time when the river is ice ask me
mistakes I have made. Ask me whether
what I have done is my life. Others
have come in their slow way into
my thought, and some have tried to help
or to hurt: ask me what difference
their strongest love or hate has made.

I will listen to what you say.
You and I can turn and look
at the silent river and wait. We know
the current is there, hidden; and there
are comings and goings from miles away
that hold the stillness exactly before us.
What the river says, that is what I say.

THE WATER

The brook had been frozen almost everywhere
    Mounds
of snow covered the ice voluptuously serene
and white as corpseflesh and quiet small sounds
came from the holes where the black skein
of water continued winding But now
only the scraps and tatters of the snow
are left on the banks and the water
seems purged of darkness brighter
than its winding immanence In the shallows
where pebbles excite the current
the brook is shaken like the quivering lightandshadow
of aspenleaves or like the cadence
of hundreds of migrant wings flashing in sunlight
against the flow forever far from their nests
and singing singing so pleasantly in their flight.

NIGHT SKATING ON THE LITTLE
PADDLE RIVER

Skinny music: needle
in its empty groove.
Our cattail torches make dark
darker but more interested in us,
gathered in velvet fists around each
halo of light. Slow
flits; we circulate as cautious
ceremonious bats.
                              Some, turning
with crossovers chick
chick chick place themselves
among the starswirl and the mix
of elements, as ice
receives the image of our torches deep within itself
and thinks.
Some may glimpse a lost one
in the spaces between skaters or the watchers,
elderly or pregnant,
by the bonfire.
And some may concentrate on carving little
crescents of this hospitable dark to carry home
and dwell on through the solitudes of daily,
perfectly legible, life.

From RIVER

The river always flows
But I stand still sometimes
As if stuck between rocks.
I try to speak
But can't say it right.
Probably because I like the river.
When being near something we like
We falter, and words don't flow.

SHUNTARŌ TANIKAWA (b. 1931)
TRANS. NAOKO ISHIKURA SMITH

THE RIVER VOYAGERS

Where the light's bells ring
Morning on the river,
Waking the town to its round of spires
And burials, is only half
The world. This very light shapes a country
Green of leaf and river
Within the sleep of the dead voyagers,
Or their death also
Is a river where morning returns
And is welcome.
The scarlet bird chanting
Its renewal in a tree of shade
As constantly sings
To their earthen unhearing ears.

The ghosts of the voyagers are gay
In the total sleep of their bones.
From the green noon shade of the river
Their vision slowly loves the sky,
Accepting bird flight, dawn and dark.
Rage for flesh and possession over,
They are gentle now. Their boats, swamped
With voyages and drowned, release the stream.
Through the broad country of their sleep,
Burnished towers and belfries of the sun,
The river runs to noon forever.
The clear light rings with bees.

EARLY DECEMBER IN
CROTON-ON-HUDSON

Spiked sun. The Hudson's
Whittled down by ice.
I hear the bone dice
Of blown gravel clicking. Bone-
pale, the recent snow
Fastens like fur to the river.
Standstill. We were leaving to deliver
Christmas presents when the tire blew
Last year. Above the dead valves pines pared
Down by a storm stood, limbs bared . . .
I want you.

I WAS SLEEPING WHERE
THE BLACK OAKS MOVE

We watched from the house
as the river grew, helpless
and terrible in its unfamiliar body.
Wrestling everything into it,
the water wrapped around trees
until their life-hold was broken.
They went down, one by one,
and the river dragged off their covering.

Nests of the herons, roots washed to bones,
snags of soaked bark on the shoreline:
a whole forest pulled through the teeth
of the spillway. Trees surfacing
singly, where the river poured off
into arteries for fields below the reservation.

When at last it was over, the long removal,
they had all become the same dry wood.
We walked among them, the branches
whitening in the raw sun.
Above us drifted herons,
alone, hoarse-voiced, broken,
settling their beaks among the hollows.
Grandpa said, *These are the ghosts of the tree people*
moving among us, unable to take their rest.

Sometimes now, we dream our way back to the
        heron dance.
Their long wings are bending the air
into circles through which they fall.
They rise again in shifting wheels.
How long must we live in the broken figures
their necks make, narrowing the sky.

LIABLE TO FLOODS

"Liable to floods" the farmer warned them.
And on the map, the letters arcing down the valley
in black and white
but still the major wouldn't listen –

tipping back his cap with one finger
and laying a fatherly hand on the farmer's shoulder
"Don't you worry Jack," he said,
"We've got this one covered."

And so they made their camp,
a thousand tents across the valley floor,
but even then as the GI's tapped the steel
they felt the backbone of the rock, shallow beneath
     the soil.

For the next two days they trained
under Moel Siabod's shoulder.
Greenhorns from Kansas, Ohio and Iowa,
sweeping in a line

through the ditches, streams and bracken,
preparing for the landings on Utah and Omaha
pegged as yet to an unknown date
hung somewhere just over the horizon.

On the third night they slept to the sound
of the rain's fusillade and the artillery of thunder,
while outside, under cover of darkness
the river pulled herself up and spread her wings,

bleeding through the camp like ink from a broken
        cartridge.
The guards were woken by their tin cans and cups
set afloat and clinking against each other
like ghosts in celebration.

They raised the alarm but it was already too late
and the river, arming herself with their rifles,
flushing out the latrines, swallowing the jeeps,
gathered them all and ushered them off.

And as their camp beds became rafts,
gently lifted and spun, more than one GI
woke from dreams of home to sense,
just for a second, somewhere deep in the bone,

how suitable this was,
as if the weather had finally caught up with their lives –
this being taken at night without any say,
this being borne, this being swept away.

PLEASURE CRAFT

Things are said.
You go on;
the going on is straight.

More things
are said.
And it goes on –

deep, slow water
south of Brantford which should make
for a relaxing day's canoeing.

Things unsaid
are said –

as you leave the city
a large curve known as the Ox-Bow
nearly turns the river back into itself.

Sodden sand, bagged.
Storm management, the gullies
overwhelmed.

After which the river continues to meander southward
with the Six Nations Indian Reservation
on the right bank.

And a number of dairy farms on the left.

KAREN HOULE (b. 1965)   123

CLONFEACLE

It happened not far away
In this meadowland
That Patrick lost a tooth.
I translate the placename

As we walk along
The river where he washed,
That translates stone to silt.
The river would preach

As well as Patrick did.
A tongue of water passing
Between teeth of stones.
Making itself clear,

Living by what it says,
Converting meadowland to marsh.
You turn towards me,
Coming round to my way

Of thinking, holding
Your tongue between your teeth.
I turn my back on the river
And Patrick, their sermons

Ending in the air.

BIRDWATCHER

The Birdwatcher moves quietly,
Seeing his way in the dark.

White-throated, splay-footed,
Sways with the reeds,
Watching the swans in their kitchens.

All night the piercing police whistle curlews
Are searching the marshes,
Keeping the river on red alert, but he kneels
Non-descript in his hide,
From headland to headland
His blue eyes glide not blinking.

He sees everything:
The grebe's nest under the weed,
The waders resting on fold-up stools along
        the tideline.

Everything down to the lowest least whisper
Of ducks tucked in self-pillow
And meals wriggling under stones,

Even the shiver of an owl's wing
Moving through stars
                    he perfectly hears . . .

At last at low water he stands up,
Remembering his heavy feet.

Now he splashes away through the heavenly
        reed fields
And the numberless pools of the Dawn . . .

Behind his back there are twenty tiny goddesses
Washing their dresses in the waves.

And the doves in the woods
Clap awake when he walks.

FLOOD PLAIN

I'd like to go on as though there's no end.
One vast

causeway to the ocean. All the
unsolved bits

as gold pressed into stone.
Solar-flash,

false capture. Sky like glass
on the water.

Here, then there, then back to a never-
again. When

the spidery clouds take up the radiance
in colors

severe with impermanence;
when the maple

along the avenue is bird-filled, a ruckus
of song and

flurry, there will be a softening,
some release:

surface winds will switch the leaves
to silver (a ripple

of creaturely breathing); snow-melt
will animate the stream; and

the grazing grounds will wash out over
broad stones.

GLACIER

The miles-deep Greenland glacier's lost its grip,
sliding nine miles a year towards the sea
on its own melt-water. As, forty years ago,
the slag-heap, loosened by a slip
of rain-swollen mountain streams, suddenly
gave with a roar, a down-hurtling flow
of spoil taking a primary school,
crushing the children. The century of waste
has burned a hole in the sky over the Pole.
Oh, science, with your tricks and alchemies,
chain the glacier with sun and wind and tide,
rebuild the gates of ice, halt melt and slide,
freeze the seas, stay the floe and the flux
for footfall of polar bear and Arctic fox.

GILLIAN CLARKE (b. 1937)

TROUBLED WATERS

Like an unseasonable stormy day,
Which makes the silver rivers drown their shores,
As if the world were all dissolv'd to tears . . .

WILLIAM SHAKESPEARE
Richard II, Act III, Scene II

When Mojaves say the word for tears, *we return*
to our word for river, *as if our river were flowing*
from our eyes. A great weeping, *is how you*
might translate it. Or, a river of grief.

NATALIE DIAZ
The First Water Is the Body

From THE EPIC OF GILGAMESH

May the sacred river Ulay mourn you,
   along whose banks we walked in our vigour!
May the pure Euphrates mourn you,
   whose water we poured in libation from skins!

Tablet VIII, 20

Ever the river has risen and brought us the flood,
   the mayfly floating on the water.
On the face of the sun its countenance gazes,
   then all of a sudden nothing is there!

Tablet X, 315

(*c.* 2100–1200 BCE)
TRANS. ANDREW GEORGE

DEAN-BOURN, A RUDE RIVER IN DEVON
by which sometimes he lived.

Dean-bourn, farewell; I never look to see
Deane, or thy warty incivility.
Thy rockie bottome, that doth teare thy streams
And makes them frantick, ev'n to all extreames;
To my content, I never sho'd behold,
Were thy streames silver, or thy rocks all gold.
Rockie thou art; and rockie we discover
Thy men; and rockie are thy wayes all over.
O men, O manners; Now, and ever knowne
To be *A Rockie Generation!*
A people currish; churlish as the seas;
And rude (almost) as rudest Salvages.
With whom I did, and may re-sojourne when
Rockes turn to Rivers, Rivers turn to Men.

WHY SHOULD I CARE FOR THE
MEN OF THAMES

Why should I care for the men of Thames,
Or the cheating waves of charter'd streams,
Or shrink at the little blasts of fear
That the hireling blows into my ear?

Tho' born on the cheating banks of Thames,
Tho' his waters bathed my infant limbs,
The Ohio shall wash his stains from me:
I was born a slave, but I go to be free.

ROLL, JORDAN, ROLL

Went down to the river Jordan,
Where John baptised three
Well I walked to the devil in hell
Sayin' John ain't baptise me
I say,
Roll, Jordan, roll
Roll, Jordan, roll

My soul arise in heaven, Lord
For the year when Jordan roll
Well some say John was a Baptist
Some say John was a Jew
But I say John was a preacher of God
And my bible says so too
I say,
Roll, Jordan, roll
Roll, Jordan, roll

My soul arise in heaven, Lord
For the year when Jordan roll
Roll, Jordan, roll
Roll, Jordan, roll
My soul arise in heaven, Lord
For the year when Jordan roll
Alleluja!
Roll, Jordan, roll
Roll, Jordan, roll

DEEP RIVER

Deep river, my home is over Jordan,
Deep river, Lord,
I want to cross over into campground.
Oh, don't you want to go to that gospel feast,
That promised land where all is peace?
Oh, deep river, Lord,
I want to cross over into campground.

CAVALRY CROSSING A FORD

A line in long array where they wind betwixt green
    islands,
They take a serpentine course, their arms flash in the
    sun – hark to the musical clank,
Behold the silvery river, in it the splashing horses
    loitering stop to drink,
Behold the brown-faced men, each group, each person
    a picture, the negligent rest on the saddles,
Some emerge on the opposite bank, others are just
    entering the ford – while,
Scarlet and blue and snowy white,
The guidon flags flutter gayly in the wind.

THE SOG, ICELAND

I sat by the Sog one morning
when sea-cold north winds blew,
looking on lands with hardly
a living thing in view.

But soon the blessèd sun rose,
sweeping the clouds away,
and worlds on worlds of creatures
woke to the newborn day.

Among them billions of blackflies
blotted the sun in murk
and swirled in swarms round Thordur
who swatted as if berserk.

JÓNAS HALLGRÍMSSON (1807–45)
TRANS. DICK RINGLER

SHADWELL STAIR

I am the ghost of Shadwell Stair.
  Along the wharves by the water-house,
  And through the dripping slaughter-house,
I am the shadow that walks there.

Yet I have flesh both firm and cool,
  And eyes tumultuous as the gems
  Of moons and lamps in the lapping Thames
When dusk sails wavering down the pool.

Shuddering the purple street-arc burns
  Where I watch always; from the banks
  Dolorously the shipping clanks,
And after me a strange tide turns.

I walk till the stars of London wane
  And dawn creeps up the Shadwell Stair.
  But when the crowing syrens blare
I with another ghost am lain.

CHARON

The conductor's hands were black with money:
Hold on to your ticket, he said, the inspector's
Mind is black with suspicion, and hold on to
That dissolving map. We moved through London,
We could see the pigeons through the glass but failed
To hear their rumours of wars, we could see
The lost dog barking but never knew
That his bark was as shrill as a cock crowing,
We just jogged on, at each request
Stop there was a crowd of aggressively vacant
Faces, we just jogged on, eternity
Gave itself airs in revolving lights
And then we came to the Thames and all
The bridges were down, the further shore
Was lost in fog, so we asked the conductor
What we should do. He said: Take the ferry
Faute de mieux. We flicked the flashlight
And there was the ferryman just as Virgil
And Dante had seen him. He looked at us coldly
And his eyes were dead and his hands on the oar
Were black with obols and varicose veins
Marbled his calves and he said to us coldly:
If you want to die you will have to pay for it.

THE GOLDEN BOAT

Clouds rumbling in the sky; teeming rain.
I sit on the river-bank, sad and alone.
The sheaves lie gathered,   harvest has ended,
The river is swollen and fierce in its flow.
As we cut the paddy it started to rain.

One small paddy-field, no one but me –
Flood-waters twisting and swirling everywhere.
Trees on the far bank   smear shadows like ink
On a village painted on deep morning grey.
On this side a paddy-field, no one but me.

Who is this, steering close to the shore,
Singing? I feel that she is someone I know.
The sails are filled wide,   she gazes ahead,
Waves break helplessly against the boat each side.
I watch and feel I have seen her face before.

Oh to what foreign land do you sail?
Come to the bank and moor your boat for a while.
Go where you want to,   give where you care to,
But come to the bank a moment, show your smile –
Take away my golden paddy when you sail.

Take it, take as much as you can load.
Is there more? No, none, I have put it aboard.
My intense labour   here by the river –
I have parted with it all, layer upon layer:
Now take me as well, be kind, take me aboard.

No room, no room, the boat is too small.
Loaded with my gold paddy, the boat is full.
Across the rain-sky   clouds heave to and fro,
On the bare river-bank, I remain alone –
What I had has gone: the golden boat took all.

RABINDRANATH TAGORE (1861–1941)
TRANS. WILLIAM RADICE

ON THE BANKS OF THE WABASH,
FAR AWAY

Round my Indiana homestead wave the cornfields,
In the distance loom the woodlands clear and cool.
Oftentimes my thoughts revert to scenes of childhood,
Where I first received my lessons, nature's school.
But one thing there is missing from the picture,
Without her face it seems so incomplete.
I long to see my mother in the doorway,
As she stood there years ago, her boy to greet.

Oh, the moonlight's fair tonight along the Wabash,
From the fields there comes the breath of
    new-mown hay.
Through the sycamores the candle lights are
    gleaming,
On the banks of the Wabash, far away.

Many years have passed since I strolled by the river,
Arm in arm, with sweetheart Mary by my side,
It was there I tried to tell her that I loved her,
It was there I begged of her to be my bride.
Long years have passed since I strolled thro' the
    churchyard.
She's sleeping there, my angel, Mary dear,
I loved her, but she thought I didn't mean it,
Still I'd give my future were she only here.

LEDA

Where the slow river
meets the tide,
a red swan lifts red wings
and darker beak,
and underneath the purple down
of his soft breast
uncurls his coral feet.

Through the deep purple
of the dying heat
of sun and mist,
the level ray of sun-beam
has caressed
the lily with dark breast,
and flecked with richer gold
its golden crest.

Where the slow lifting
of the tide,
floats into the river
and slowly drifts
among the reeds,
and lifts the yellow flags,
he floats
where tide and river meet.

Ah kingly kiss —
no more regret
nor old deep memories
to mar the bliss;
where the low sedge is thick,
the gold day-lily
outspreads and rests
beneath soft fluttering
of red swan wings
and the warm quivering
of the red swan's breast.

From PATERSON

Paterson lies in the valley under the Passaic
    Falls
its spent waters forming the outline of his
        back. He
lies on his right side, head near the thunder
of the waters filling his dreams! Eternally
        asleep,
his dreams walk about the city where he
        persists
incognito. Butterflies settle on his stone ear.
Immortal he neither moves nor rouses and is
        seldom
seen, though he breathes and subtleties of his
        machinations
drawing their substance from the noise of the
        pouring river
animate a thousand automatons. Who because
        they
neither know their sources nor the sills of
        their
disappointments walk outside their bodies
        aimlessly for the most part,
locked and forgot in their desires – unroused.

– Say it, no ideas but in things –
nothing but the blank faces of the houses
and cylindrical trees

   bent, forked by preconception and accident –
split, furrowed, creased, mottled, stained –
secret – into the body of the light!

From above, higher than the spires, higher
even than the office towers, from oozy fields
abandoned to grey beds of dead grass,

From OL' MAN RIVER

Dere's an ol' man called de Mississippi
Dat's de ol' man dat I'd like to be
What does he care if de world's got troubles
What does he care if de land ain't free

Ol' man river, dat ol' man river
He mus' know sumpin', but don't say nuthin'
He jes' keeps rollin'
He keeps on rollin' along

He don' plant taters, he don't plant cotton
An' dem dat plants 'em is soon forgotten
But ol' man river
He jes' keeps rollin' along

You an' me, we sweat an' strain
Body all achin' an' wracked wid pain,
Tote dat barge! Lif' dat bale!
Git a little drunk an' you lands in jail

Ah gits weary an' sick of tryin'
Ah'm tired of livin' an' skeered of dyin'
But ol' man river
He jes' keeps rollin' along

OSCAR HAMMERSTEIN II (1895–1960)   149

THE RIVER

Even here we have driven the river underground.
Not because we didn't admire its icy clarity,
Like glass, that scarcely bent the light of the sun;
Or because we didn't want to refresh ourselves
At its bubbling fountain,
Or bathe in it, where it purled over the stones
Singing to itself its endless song;
Not because it didn't water the plain
And carry off our refuse, washing away
The traces of our picnic on the planet;
I have seen it race like a black torrent
Down the steep channel of the street.
I have heard it roaring under the rain,
And searched for it through the dry days, hoping
For a token to show it would return.
But now it is buried under pavingstones
Deep in the rocks from which it sprang.
In the darkness it hisses and mutters, feeling its way
Like a blind man on an unfamiliar street
Tapping his path between strangers.

THE RIVER GOD

I may be smelly and I may be old,
Rough in my pebbles, reedy in my pools,
But where my fish float by I bless their swimming
And I like the people to bathe in me, especially
     women.
But I can drown the fools
Who bathe too close to the weir, contrary to rules.
And they take a long time drowning
As I throw them up now and then in a spirit of
     clowning.
Hi yih, yippity-yap, merrily I flow,
O I may be an old foul river but I have plenty of go.
Once there was a lady who was too bold
She bathed in me by the tall black cliff where the
     water runs cold,
So I brought her down here
To be my beautiful dear.
Oh will she stay with me will she stay
This beautiful lady, or will she go away?
She lies in my beautiful deep river bed with many
     a weed
To hold her, and many a waving reed.
Oh who would guess what a beautiful white face lies
     there
Waiting for me to smooth and wash away the fear
She looks at me with. Hi yih, do not let her
Go. There is no one on earth who does not forget her

Now. They say I am a foolish old smelly river
But they do not know of my wide original bed
Where the lady waits, with her golden sleepy head.
If she wishes to go I will not forgive her.

OPHELIA

Where the pool unfurls its undercloud –
There she goes

And through and through
The kneading tumble and the water-hammer.

If a trout leaps into air, it is not for a breather.
It has to drop back immediately

Into this peculiar engine
That made it and keeps it going

And that works it to death –
                            there she goes

Darkfish, finger to her lips,
Staringly into the afterworld.

RISING DAMP
(*for C.A.K. and R.K.M.*)

"A river can sometimes be diverted, but it is a very hard thing to lose it altogether." (J. G. Head: *paper read to the Auctioneers' Institute in 1907*)

At our feet they lie low,
The little fervent underground
Rivers of London

Effra, Graveney, Falcon, Quaggy,
Wandle, Walbrook, Tyburn, Fleet

Whose names are disfigured,
Frayed, effaced.

These are the Magogs that chewed the clay
To the basin that London nestles in.
These are the currents that chiselled the city,
That washed the clothes and turned the mills,
Where children drank and salmon swam
And wells were holy.

They have gone under.
Boxed, like the magician's assistant.
Buried alive in earth.
Forgotten, like the dead.

They return spectrally after heavy rain,
Confounding suburban gardens. They infiltrate
Chronic bronchitis statistics. A silken
Slur haunts dwellings by shrouded
Watercourses, and is taken
For the footing of the dead.

Being of our world, they will return
(Westbourne, caged at Sloane Square,
Will jack from his box),
Will deluge cellars, detonate manholes,
Plant effluent on our faces,
Sink the city.

Effra, Graveney, Falcon, Quaggy,
Wandle, Walbrook, Tyburn, Fleet

It is the other rivers that lie
Lower, that touch us only in dreams
That never surface. We feel their tug
As a dowser's rod bends to the source below

Phlegethon, Acheron, Lethe, Styx.

RIVER

On the road, whenever I rose
        there was no one.
Along the way, wanting a friend,
        no one joined me.

Alone I traveled in foreign circles
        and had to fit in,
gaining entry, garnering little-by-little
        prestige in their eyes.

Lakes couldn't corner me
        nor mountains block me.
My self-assurance frightened them.
        Unable to bully me, they gave up.

Still, some witless so-called men
        harassed me
as if progressive ways
        were found under rocks, or in trees.

Worn down by life's sorrows,
        I'm unable to be worldly.
Unable to understand me,
        they say I'm *escapist*.

Reaching now my beloved ocean
       To behold it! There!
The fire beneath the sea
       remains, tranquil and patient.

As I reach the end, he smiles
       comforting me with his love.
It's time I go, why keep him waiting?
       So what if they call me *coward*!

CITTADHAR HṚDAYA (1906–82)
TRANS. DAVID HARGREAVES

AT THE CONFLUENCE OF
THE COLORADO AND
THE LITTLE COLORADO

Where the two rivers come together – one cold,
one desert-warm – the party beached the raft
    to swim.
A blue aileron, looking new, lay on the bank
and Dennis put his shirt and bluejeans in it,
out of the wind that had blown his hat away.
Across the canyon, silver in the sun,
the fuselage glinted. The wreck was ten years old,
two liners that had come together in broad day,
dropping their metal feathers,
and two tribes of travellers who settled then
where the wind told them to settle.

To that lost Indian tribe, who farmed this dry
    grandeur once,
they might have seemed to be surrogates of gods
(anything but gods, these downcast mortals,
anything but wrathful, they fell bemused
at various unfulfillments, at sheer bad luck)
as they descended, shorn of all human gear
and taking what they found: the shimmering
    desert air,
white water, the hot shale.
                      And the hectoring solitude

that now made the rafters douse and romp
      and chatter,
a solitude that reverts to the subject of death
whenever the conversation of live things lags.

THE RIVERS

the rivers of hell are mine, they aren't yours,
they're mine, flowing hot and dirty and
endless,
they're mine, all mine,
special,
for me,
nobody else,
they're mine
rushing me along,
night and day,
week after week, month after month,
year after year,
they're mine,
you hear me?

I no longer try to climb out,
I go with the rivers,
I talk to the rivers,
I tell them things
like,
"I know you.
we've been together a long
time.
I expect nothing
else."

we rush toward death
and neither of us
gives a damn about
death,
we've got our own game
going.

the rivers of hell are mine,
mine,
the rivers of hell
flowing
moving
with me,
my hells can only be
my hells,
if they're mine now and
maybe
forever,
so be
it.

LIMPOPO BLUES

I am not swimming across this river. I am reading
a headline in the free newspaper on the plane: *17
Zimbabweans drown in Limpopo River.* I do not call my
cousin-brothers in Cape Town when I touch down in
Jozi for the conference, in case they want bus fare to
come visit me, or sound flat when I mention my book,
or notice that I ask about their little one, but not
by name. What a croc, this river between rand and
dollar, and neither one ours. This river has double-
crossed us.

THE RIVER

The city is one. A dirty river cuts it in 2: swamp of
sweats. The poetry is many: words transmute as soon
as you cross this river. A gaze scrutinizes from the
bushes the green passage from the water. Here is the
end of the closed heart, the end of an orphan country;
here other meanings begin.

The red river separates the city and in each universe
puts together its history of *fiesta* or nightmare.
As soon as the border is transposed, the same voice
prays other realities. From this shore there is blood
over the stones and the gun still looks for its target:
skin bathed in lean moons against the whistle
of metal. But the city is only one.

There is a black river flowing through the middle
of the city, a river armed of night between antlers
of the buildings. It divides the city in black and white.
The south is a scream; the north a party of light.
This river goes forward under the bridges like a
dagger reaping cotton fields. The city hurts and sings,
but under the sunlight it is only one.

JORGE HUMBERTO CHÁVEZ (b. 1959)
TRANS. JAIME MARROQUÍN ARREDONDO   163

WADE IN THE WATER
for the Geechee Gullah Ring Shouters

One of the women greeted me.
I love you, she said. She didn't
Know me, but I believed her,
And a terrible new ache
Rolled over in my chest,
Like in a room where the drapes
Have been swept back. I love you,
I love you, as she continued
Down the hall past other strangers,
Each feeling pierced suddenly
By pillars of heavy light.
I love you, throughout
The performance, in every
Handclap, every stomp.
I love you in the rusted iron
Chains someone was made
To drag until love let them be
Unclasped and left empty
In the center of the ring.
I love you in the water
Where they pretended to wade,
Singing that old blood-deep song
That dragged us to those banks
And cast us in. I love you,
The angles of it scraping at
Each throat, shouldering past

The swirling dust motes
In those beams of light
That whatever we now knew
We could let ourselves feel, knew
To climb. O Woods – O Dogs –
O Tree – O Gun – O *Girl, run* –
O Miraculous Many Gone –
O Lord – O Lord – O Lord –
Is this love the trouble you promised?

RIVERBED BLUES

Early mornings, before leaving
to labor long hours, my father
painted rivers at our kitchen table.
Hammer-hardened hands guided
brushes full of blues over banks
and stones. He was drowning
on those banks, I know.

On days I should have been reading,
feeding my waterlogged brain,
paddling ducks and slippery rocks
sat substitute for Ben Franklin's virtues.
Drinking beer, yanking bluegill from
beneath lily-pad lies with a cheap pole
bought by burger money.

The first four I freed, each slipping
gently between wet hands back to
cool shadows. The fifth glittering bream
didn't make it there, left hooked
to flop brilliant flashes of desperation.
Drown with me, Blue.
I was that lonely.

MEDITATIONS &
MEANDERINGS

You cannot step twice into the same river, for other waters are continually flowing on.

HERACLITUS

The river is everywhere at once, at its source and at its mouth, at the waterfall, at the ferry, at the rapids, in the sea, in the mountains, everywhere at once, and only the present exists for it, and not the shadow of the future.

HERMANN HESSE
Siddhartha

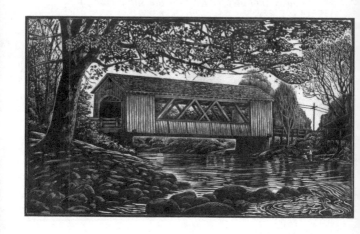

From DAO DE JIN

Nothing in the world is softer and weaker than water,
And yet, when attacking the strong and hard,
    nothing prevails like water.
Nothing can improve water or take its place.
The weak overcomes the strong, the soft overcomes
    the hard.
Everyone in the world knows this,
yet no one can put this principle into practice.

Chapt. LXXVII

LAOZI (*fl.* 550 BCE)
TRANS. JIN LEI

THOUGHTS ON TRAVELING BY NIGHT

Light wind rippling the grassy shore,
The high mast of a lone boat in the night,
Stars hanging low over the wide plain,
The moon flows with the great river.
So much writing without any fame,
Growing old and sick, I retire from my post.
Floating and drifting – what is my likeness?
A lonesome gull between Heaven and Earth.

DU FU (712–70)
170   TRANS. JIN LEI

CRICKET SINGING

On a branch
Swept down river,
A cricket singing

KOBAYASHI ISSA (1763 – 1828)
TRANS. NAOKO ISHIKURA SMITH

BELOW THE JUMPING SWEETFISH

Below the jumping sweetfish
Along the stream bed
Clouds are sailing

UEJIMA ONITSURA (1661 – 1738)
TRANS. NAOKO ISHIKURA SMITH

UPON WESTMINSTER BRIDGE
Sept. 3, 1802

Earth has not anything to show more fair:
    Dull would he be of soul who could pass by
    A sight so touching in its majesty:
This City now doth, like a garment, wear
The beauty of the morning; silent, bare,
    Ships, towers, domes, theatres, and temples lie
    Open unto the fields, and to the sky;
All bright and glittering in the smokeless air.
Never did sun more beautifully steep
    In his first splendour, valley, rock, or hill;
Ne'er saw I, never felt, a calm so deep!
    The river glideth at his own sweet will:
Dear God! the very houses seem asleep;
    And all that mighty heart is lying still!

SYMPHONY IN YELLOW

An omnibus across the bridge
   Crawls like a yellow butterfly,
   And, here and there, a passer-by
Shows like a little restless midge.

Big barges full of yellow hay
   Are moved against the shadowy wharf,
   And, like a yellow silken scarf,
The thick fog hangs along the quay.

The yellow leaves begin to fade
   And flutter from the Temple elms,
   And at my feet the pale green Thames
Lies like a rod of rippled jade.

OSCAR WILDE (1854–1900)   173

THE CARAFES OF THE VIVONNE

In the summer I enjoyed watching
The carafes in the Vivonne
Village boys put there to catch minnows.

Filled by the river, the glass bottles became
At once clear-sided containers, like hardened water,
And themselves contained by that larger container
The Vivonne, made of crystal, fluid and flowing;
They evoked an image of coolness
In a way more delicious and more
Frustrating than their domestic counterparts
Awaiting guests *à table.*

For the river revealed them ever fleeing,
Endlessly repeating twinned escapes,
Back and forth, between flowing water and
    fixed glass,
What the hand cannot hold and
Where the tongue tastes no pleasure.

MARCEL PROUST (1871–1922)
TRANS. KIT ANDREWS

MIRABEAU BRIDGE

Beneath the Mirabeau Bridge flows the Seine
     And our loves
   Must I remember them
Joy always followed pain

       The night draws in, the hour rings
       Days depart, I stay

Hand in hand, let's remain face-to-face
     Whilst waters wearied by our eternal gaze
   Pass under
Our bridge of arms

       The night draws in, the hour rings
       Days depart, I stay

Love leaves like the flowing waters
     Love slips away
   How slow life is
And how fierce our hope

       The night draws in, the hour rings
       Days depart, I stay

Days go by, weeks go by
    Neither the olden days
  Nor the loves of old will pass again
Beneath the Mirabeau Bridge flows the Seine

    The night draws in, the hour rings
    Days depart, I stay

GUILLAUME APOLLINAIRE (1880–1918)
176 TRANS. CHLOË HUGHES

THE RIVER OF RIVERS
IN CONNECTICUT

There is a great river this side of Stygia,
Before one comes to the first black cataracts
And trees that lack the intelligence of trees.

In that river, far this side of Stygia,
The mere flowing of the water is a gayety.
Flashing and flashing in the sun. On its banks,

No shadow walks. The river is fateful,
Like the last one. But there is no ferryman.
He could not bend against its propelling force.

It is not to be seen beneath the appearances
That tell of it. The steeple at Farmington
Stands glistening and Haddam shines and sways.

It is the third commonness with light and air,
A curriculum, a vigor, a local abstraction . . .
Call it, once more, a river, an unnamed flowing,

Space-filled, reflecting the seasons, the folk-lore
Of each of the senses; call it, again and again,
The river that flows nowhere, like a sea.

WALLACE STEVENS (1879–1955)   177

THE NEGRO SPEAKS OF RIVERS

I've known rivers:
I've known rivers ancient as the world and older than
    the flow of human blood in human veins.

My soul has grown deep like the rivers.

I bathed in the Euphrates when dawns were young.
I built my hut near the Congo and it lulled me
    to sleep.
I looked upon the Nile and raised the pyramids
    above it.
I heard the singing of the Mississippi when Abe
    Lincoln went down to New Orleans, and I've
    seen its muddy bosom turn all golden in the
    sunset.

I've known rivers:
Ancient, dusky rivers.

My soul has grown deep like the rivers.

THE RIVER BENDS BUT THE WATER DOES NOT

The river bends – water itself does not
Don't deceive, be considered, use reason
Body and mind are pure, straightforward,
Yet desire and all trickery are twisted

A pure mind consists of light
A desire is overcome and shattered
Desire like the river shifts and turns
The mind like water does not bend

The mind can be calm though the body quickens
It's no trick that in turbid rivers there's clear water
And in mercy there is enough of Nirvana
Everything that bewilders leads to questions

The Monk said cut the forest, not the trees
I don't know how one can try to log like that
They say that to be deemed wise
You must know how to find the water in the river

BUDDHADĀSA BHIKKHU (1906–93)
TRANS. ROBERT A. TROYER and
DYLAN J. HARTMANN

POURING THE SAND MANDALA
INTO THE THAMES

I still hear them –
the Buddhist monks
rasping their cones
of coloured sand

the mandala falling
in a fine stream,
the river wearing
its oiled silks.

It forces the flow –
the treachery of images –
the briar that blooms
as if unpremeditated

then bewilders the bone.

FAUN

Haunched like a faun, he hooed
From grove of moon-glint and fen-frost
Until all owls in the twigged forest
Flapped black to look and brood
On the call this man made.

No sound but a drunken coot
Lurching home along river bank.
Stars hung water-sunk, so a rank
Of double star-eyes lit
Boughs where those owls sat.

An arena of yellow eyes
Watched the changing shape he cut,
Saw hoof harden from foot, saw sprout
Goat-horns. Marked how god rose
And galloped woodward in that guise.

BY THE RIVER EDEN

1

Never twice that river
Though the still turning water
In its dark pools
Mirrors suspended green
Of an unchanging scene.

Frail bubbles revolve,
Break in the rippling falls,
The same, I could believe,
Each with its moment gone,
I watched in former years,

Ever-reforming maze
Of evening midge's dance,
Swifts that chase and scream
Touching in their low flight
The picture on the stream.

Heart is deceived,
Or knows what mind ignores:
Not the mirroring flux
Nor mirrored scene remain
Nor the rocky bed
Of the river's course,

But shadows intangible
That fade and come again.
Through their enduring forms
The glassy river runs;
All flows save the image
Cast on that shimmering screen.

2

Beside the river Eden
Some child has made her secret garden
On an alder strand
Marked out with pebbles in the sand,
Patterned with meadow flowers,
As once I did, and was.

My mother who from time past
Recalls the red spots on the yellow mimulus
That nodded in the burn
To her alone
Was that same child,

And hers, bedridden,
Mused on an old cracked darkened picture of a
        salmon-river
Painted in Paradise so long ago
None living ever saw those tumbling waters flow.
By her imagination made miraculous
Water of life poured over its faded varnished stones.

All is one, I or another,
She was I, she was my mother,
The same child for ever
Building the same green bower by the same river.

3

The lapwing's wavering flight
Warns me from her nest,
Her wild sanctuary;
Dark wings, white breast.
The Nine Nicks have weathered,
Lichened slabs tumbled,
In sand under roots of thyme
Bone and feather lie,
The ceaseless wind has blown;
But over my gray head
The plover's unageing cry.

DRIVING TOWARD THE LAC QUI PARLE RIVER

I

I am driving; it is dusk; Minnesota.
The stubble field catches the last growth of sun.
The soybeans are breathing on all sides.
Old men are sitting before their houses on carseats
In the small towns. I am happy,
The moon rising above the turkey sheds.

II

The small world of the car
Plunges through the deep fields of the night,
On the road from Willmar to Milan.
This solitude covered with iron
Moves through the fields of night
Penetrated by the noise of crickets.

III

Nearly to Milan, suddenly a small bridge,
And water kneeling in the moonlight.
In small towns the houses are built right on the
    ground;
The lamplight falls on all fours in the grass.
When I reach the river, the full moon falls on it;
A few people are talking low in a boat.

ROBERT BLY (1926–2021)   185

HENLEY-ON-THAMES

I see the winding water make
A short and then a shorter lake
    As here stand I,
    And house-boat high
Survey the Upper Thames.
  By sun the mud is amber-dyed
  In ripples slow and flat and wide,
  That flap against the house-boat side
And flop away in gems.

In mud and elder-scented shade
A reach away the breach is made
    By dive and shout
    That circles out
To Henley tower and town;
  And "Boats for Hire" the rafters ring,
  And pink on white the roses cling,
  And red the bright geraniums swing
In baskets dangling down.

When shall I see the Thames again?
The prow-promoted gems again,
    As beefy ATS
    Without their hats
Come shooting through the bridge?
  And "cheerioh" and "cheeri-bye"
  Across the waste of waters die,
  And low the mists of evening lie
And lightly skims the midge.

SUDDENLY THERE'S POUGHKEEPSIE

what a hard time
the Hudson River has had
trying to get to the sea
it seemed easy enough to
rise out of Tear of
the Cloud and tumble
and run in little skips
and jumps   draining
         a swamp here and
   there   acquiring
streams and other smaller
rivers with similar
longings for the wide
imagined water
suddenly
there's Poughkeepsie
except for its spelling
an ordinary town but
the great heaving
ocean sixty miles away is
determined to reach
that town every day
and twice a day   in fact
drowning the Hudson River
in salt and mud
it is the moon's tidal
power over all the waters

of this earth at war with
gravity   the Hudson
perseveres   moving down
down   dignified
slower   look it has
become our Lordly Hudson
hardly flowing

                              and we are
now in a poem by the poet
Paul Goodman   be quiet heart
home home
                    then the sea

TO THE AVON RIVER, ABOVE
STRATFORD, CANADA

What did the Indians call you?
For you do not flow
With English accents.
I hardly know
What I should call you
      Because before
I drank coffee or tea
I drank you
      With my cupped hands
And you did not taste English to me
      And you do not sound
      Like Avon
      Or swans & bards
But rather like the sad wild fowl
      In prints drawn
      By Audubon
And like dear bad poets
      Who wrote
      Early in Canada
And never were of note
You are the first river
      I crossed
And like the first whirlwind
      The first rainbow
      First snow, first
      Falling star I saw,

You, for other rivers are my law.
        These other rivers:
        The Red & the Thames
        Are never so sweet
To skate upon, swim in
        Or for baptism of sin.
        Silver and light
The sentence of your voice,
        With a soprano
Continuous cry you shall
        Always flow
        Through my heart
The rain and the snow of my mind
Shall supply the spring of that river
        Forever.
Though not your name
Your coat of arms I know
        And motto:
A shield of reeds and cresses
        Sedges, crayfishes
The hermaphroditic leech
Minnows, muskrats and farmers' geese
And printed above this shield
One of my earlier wishes
"To flow like you."

RIVER IN THE VALLEY

We cross the Sacramento River at Colusa
follow the road on the levee south and east
find thousands of swallows nesting
on the underside of a concrete overhead
roadway? causeway? abandoned. Near
                           Butte Creek.

    Gen runs in little circles looking up
    at swoops of swallows – laughing –
             they keep
    flowing under the bridge and out,

    Kai leans silent against a concrete pier
    tries to hold with his eyes the course
    of a single darting bird,

    I pick grass seeds from my socks.

The coast range. Parched yellow front hills,
blue-gray thornbrush higher hills behind,
and here is the Great Central Valley,

drained, then planted and watered,
    thousand-foot deep soils
    thousand-acre orchards

    Sunday morning,
only one place serving breakfast
in Colusa, old river and tractor men
sipping milky coffee.

From north of Sutter Buttes
we see snow on Mt. Lassen
and the clear arc of the Sierra
south to the Desolation peaks.
One boy asks, "where do rivers start?"

in threads in hills, and gather down to here –
but the river
is all of it everywhere,
all flowing at once,
all one place.

ANNA LIFFEY

Life, the story goes,
Was the daughter of Canaan,
And came to the plain of Kildare.
She loved the flat-lands and the ditches
And the unreachable horizon.
She asked that it be named for her.
The river took its name from the land.
The land took its name from a woman.

A woman in the doorway of a house.
A river in the city of her birth.

There, in the hills above my house,
The river Liffey rises, is a source.
It rises in rush and ling heather and
Black peat and bracken and strengthens
To claim the city it narrated.
Swans. Steep falls. Small towns.
The smudged air and bridges of Dublin.

Dusk is coming.
Rain is moving east from the hills.

If I could see myself
I would see

A woman in a doorway
Wearing the colours that go with red hair.
Although my hair is no longer red.

I praise
The gifts of the river.
Its shiftless and glittering
Re-telling of a city,
Its clarity as it flows,
In the company of runt flowers and herons,
Around a bend at Islandbridge
And under thirteen bridges to the sea.
Its patience at twilight –
Swans nesting by it,
Neon wincing into it.

Maker of
Places, remembrances,
Narrate such fragments for me:

One body. One spirit.
One place. One name.
The city where I was born.
The river that runs through it.
The nation which eludes me.

Fractions of a life
It has taken me a lifetime
To claim.

I came here in a cold winter.

I had no children. No country.
I did not know the name for my own life.

My country took hold of me.
My children were born.

I walked out in a summer dusk
To call them in.

One name. Then the other one.
The beautiful vowels sounding out home.

Make of a nation what you will
Make of the past
What you can –

There is now
A woman in a doorway.

It has taken me
All my strength to do this.

Becoming a figure in a poem.

Usurping a name and a theme.

A river is not a woman.
    Although the names it finds,
        The history it makes
And suffers –
    The Viking blades beside it,
        The muskets of the Redcoats,
            The flames of the Four Courts
Blazing into it
    Are a sign.
        Any more than
A woman is a river,
    Although the course it takes,
        Through swans courting and distraught
            willows,
Its patience
    Which is also its powerlessness,
        From Callary to Islandbridge,
            And from source to mouth,
Is another one.
            And in my late forties

Past believing
    Love will heal
        What language fails to know
And needs to say –
    What the body means –
        I take this sign
And I make this mark:
    A woman in the doorway of her house.
        A river in the city of her birth.
The truth of a suffered life.
    The mouth of it.

The seabirds come in from the coast
The city wisdom is they bring rain.
I watch them from my doorway.
I see them as arguments of origin –
Leaving a harsh force on the horizon
Only to find it
Slanting and falling elswhere.

Which water –
The one they live or the one they pronounce –
Remembers the other?

I am sure
The body of an ageing woman
Is a memory
And to find a language for it
Is as hard
As weeping and requiring
These birds to cry out as if they could
Recognize their element
Remembered and diminished in
A single tear.

An ageing woman
Finds no shelter in language.
She finds instead
Single words she once loved
Such as "summer" and "yellow"
And "sexual" and "ready"
Have suddenly become dwellings
For someone else —
Rooms and a roof under which someone else
Is welcome, not her. Tell me,
Anna Liffey,
Spirit of water,
Spirit of place,
How is it on this
Rainy Autumn night

As the Irish sea takes
The names you made, the names
You bestowed, and gives you back
Only wordlessness?

Autumn rain is
Scattering and dripping
From car-ports
And clipped hedges.
The gutters are full.

When I came here
I had neither
Children nor country.
The trees were arms.
The hills for dreams.

I was free
To imagine a spirit
In the blues and greens,
The hills and fogs
Of a small city.

My children were born.
My country took hold of me.
A vision in a brick house.

Is it only love
That makes a place?

I feel it change.
My children are
Growing up, getting older.
My country holds on
To its own pain.

I turn off
The harsh yellow
Porch light and
Stand in the hall.
Where is home now?

Follow the rain
Out to the Dublin hills.
Let it become the river.
Let the spirit of place be
A lost soul again.

In the end
It will not matter
That I was a woman. I am sure of it.
The body is a source. Nothing more.
There is a time for it. There is a certainty

About the way it seeks its own dissolution.
Consider rivers.
They are always en route to
Their own nothingness. From the first moment
They are going home. And so
When language cannot do it for us,
Cannot make us know love will not diminish us,
There are these phrases
Of the ocean
To console us.
Particular and unafraid of their completion.
In the end
Everything that burdened and distinguished me
Will be lost in this:
I was a voice.

AT BLACK RIVER

All day
    its dark, slick bronze soaks
        in a mossy place,
            its teeth,

a multitude
    set
        for the comedy
            that never comes –

its tail
    knobbed and shiny,
        and with a heavyweight's punch
            packed around the bone.

In beautiful Florida
    he is king
        of his own part
            of the black river,

and from his nap
    he will wake
        into the warm darkness
            to boom, and thrust forward,

paralyzing
   the swift, thin-waisted fish,
      or the bird
         in its frilled, white gown,

that has dipped down
   from the heaven of leaves
      one last time,
         to drink.

Don't think
   I'm not afraid.
      There is such an unleashing
         of horror.

Then I remember:
   death comes before
      the rolling away
         of the stone.

A SNAPSHOT OF SUSITNA

Rising in a creamy glow
through blue-black night
beneath the eyes of stars,
her feline curves
classic and mature,
she shifts, she sighs;
gentle,
white-skinned lovely
under silken sheets
of winter snow she sleeps
with the odd, peaceful smile
of eternal satisfaction
as attends the lips
of an ageless lover
when the full moon drifts
across the rim of the sky.

SAM HAMILL (1943—2018)

THE WAKING FATHER

My father and I are catching spricklies
Out of the Oona river.
They have us feeling righteous,
The way we have thrown them back.
Our benevolence is astounding.

When my father stood out in the shallows
It occurred to me that
The spricklies might have been piranhas,
The river a red carpet
Rolling out from where he had just stood,

Or I wonder now if he is dead or sleeping.
For if he is dead I would have his grave
Secret and safe,
I would turn the river out of its course,
Lay him in its bed, bring it round again.

No one would question
That he had treasures or his being a king,
Telling now of the real fish farther down.

From DART

And then I saw the river's dream-self walk
down to the ringmesh netting by the bridge
to feel the edge of shingle brush the edge
of sleep and float a world up like a cork
out of its body's liquid dark.
Like in a waterfall one small twig caught
catches a stick, a straw, a sack, a mesh
of leaves, a fragile wickerwork of floodbrash,
I saw all things catch and reticulate
into this dreaming of the Dart
that sinks like a feather falls, not quite
in full possession of its weight

I wake wide in a swim of
seagulls, scavengers, monomaniac, mad
rubbish pickers, mating blatantly, screaming

and slouch off scumming and flashing and
        hatching flies
to the milk factory, staring at routine things . . .

have you forgotten the force that orders the
        world's fields
and sets all cities in their sites, this nomad
pulling the sun and moon, placeless in all places,
born with her stones, with her circular bird-voice,
carrying everywhere her quarters?

ALICE OSWALD (b. 1966)   207

BRUSH FIRE

The fire the river that's to say
the sea to drink following the sand
the feet and the hands
inside the heart to love
this river that inhabits me repeoples me
around the fire I only said to you
my race
it flows here and there a river
the flames are the gaze
of those who hold its convent
I said to you my race
she remembers
the bronze content drunk hot.

TCHICAYA U TAM'SI (1931–88)
TRANS. RYAN TOPPER

GNOSIS

In a blue river made of snowmelt
that forms this valley of aspen and alder,

I fish with my sons until summer's light fades
in the recesses of a canyon.

While hunting alone I entered a small cave
to take shelter from a passing squall

and found the bones of a bear cub
curled in a circle of trust.

Someday when the white fields disappear
and only rain falls from the heavens,

this river will vanish too.
The trout we catch have throats that shine

with a bright red mark, suggesting the role
blood plays in betrayal.

A woman who is long dead told me
that when a river passes away, it holds

the memory of itself in the silt left behind.
When our species is extinct,

what animal will carry the memory
of our lives?

TODD DAVIS (b. 1965)   209

LA SEINE

Juin

The river in front almost black,
blue further along, true blue one can never
walk to, then white where I can barely
see, it escapes into ideas of Heaven.

What work has been done,
with both hands, pleasure and pain, but real
is the pain, and kept, book of days,
with pleasure an ephemeral sigh.

Jealousy of what celebrates itself
immense, the *thingness* of the orange peels
that are everywhere, *I can clean toilets,*
a woman, passing, says.

I like the modest mosses, expressive
between stones, their tender soothings,
while a bruise-colored pigeon pillows into
sleep atop its own bosom.

Novembre

Two mallards ride like tourists upon waves
the boats make continuous.

As fogged in as voices become during medicated
sleep, when the dream incorporates them.

The sky a seagull gray-and-white, but smudged
beyond recognition.

Thus the seagull at river's edge is intense:
the clouds boil down to it.

Studded spires spike the nearness and distance.
Even their weathervanes do not choose.

Leaves the yellow of aging lemons, or green as . . .
The top branches concede their losses.

On cobblestones, horse droppings.
Hay is the affection that breaks them into gold.

DELTAS

All the rivers run into the sea,
Yet the sea is not full,
To the place from which the rivers come,
There they return again

ECCLESIASTES, 1:7

MOONLIGHT ON THE SPRING RIVER

The spring river swells level with the sea,
A brilliant moon rises with the tide,
Rippling and shining for miles and miles.
Where there's a river, there's a bright moon.
The river winds across fragrant meadows.
Moonlight, like snow, on the wooded grove.
You cannot tell moonbeams from frost,
Nor from the white sand of the riverbank.
The moonlit sky and dustless river are one.
Alone, the brilliant moon shines down.

ZHANG RUOXU (660–720)
TRANS. JIN LEI

MOGAMI RIVER

May rain
Gathered and flowing fast –
Mogami River

HOT SUMMER DAY

The Mogami River
Has poured the hot summer sun
Into the ocean

MATSUO BASHO (1644–94)
TRANS. NAOKO ISHIKURA SMITH

MY RIVER RUNS TO THEE

My River runs to thee –
Blue Sea! Wilt welcome me?
My River waits reply –
Oh Sea – look graciously –
I'll fetch thee Brooks
From spotted nooks –
Say – Sea – Take *Me*!

LEAST RIVERS

Least Rivers – docile to some sea.
My Caspian – thee.

EMILY DICKINSON (1830–86)   217

From THE RIVER COLUMBIA

Rolled up the huge gorge long a billowy roar
Has shaken the mountain firs with storms of sound;
But now the Cascades, as the bluff ye round,
Burst forth like a magnificent meteor,
Grand the white turbulence, the foamy smother,
And beautiful the blue-green stream behind,
Made less crystalline by nor wave nor wind,
As if – the one contiguous to the other –
The calm slept dead and the storm surged on ocean.
Careers, like scud before a hurricane.
The vast foam, – the great mountains whirl, –
     your brain
Reels with the rushing parallactic motion.
Look up, where flows the river gentliest,
There is a charm of peace – lo! all again is rest!

Proud Bird, with no compeer and no companion,
From where snow-summits highest are and hoarest
To where the slow swell lifts the ocean-kelp,
The river rolled in cataract through the cañon
Or seaward floating wrecks of vast fir forest,
High o'er the raven's croak, the sea-gull's yelp,
Bald Eagle of the Oregon, thou soarest!
And thou that here thy tides and billows pourest,
Calm and as strong as Heaven, sublime Pacific,
Here where the freighted inland waters launch –
Where'er the bird screams or the salt air pipes,

Ocean and Eagle, ye are Freedom's types;
When all her broad domain is beatific,
And her uncrimsoned conquering bears the
    olive branch!

THE VISITING SEA

As the inhastening tide doth roll,
Home from the deep, along the whole
   Wide shining strand, and floods the caves,
   – Your love comes filling with happy waves
The open sea-shore of my soul.

But inland from the seaward spaces,
None knows, not even you, the places
   Brimmed, at your coming, out of sight,
   – The little solitudes of delight
This tide constrains in dim embraces.

You see the happy shore, wave-rimmed,
But know not of the quiet dimmed
   Rivers your coming floods and fills,
   The little pools 'mid happier hills,
My silent rivulets, over-brimmed.

What! I have secrets from you? Yes.
But, visiting Sea, your love doth press
   And reach in further than you know,
   And fills all these; and, when you go,
There's loneliness in loneliness.

TO MYSELF

I'd love to meander as a river
Over broad, juicy meadows,
To lose myself amid the reeds,
Smiling to celestial lights.

Curving around ancient villages,
Napping by wooded hills,
To roll like a happy road
Toward the cities' youthful fuss.

Lifting ships and boats,
In joy and labor,
These waves, free and bright,
Will flow into infinite space.

But I fear that the salty space
Holds only a dream, the dream of being.
Even after death, at sea,
I want to sense my free *self.*

VALERY BRYUSOV (1873–1924)
TRANS. A. MOLOTKOV

REPOSE OF RIVERS

The willows carried a slow sound,
A sarabande the wind mowed on the mead.
I could never remember
That seething, steady leveling of the marshes
Till age had brought me to the sea.

Flags, weeds. And remembrance of steep alcoves
Where cypresses shared the noon's
Tyranny; they drew me into hades almost.
And mammoth turtles climbing sulphur dreams
Yielded, while sun-silt rippled them
Asunder . . .

How much I would have bartered! the black gorge
And all the singular nestings in the hills
Where beavers learn stitch and tooth.
The pond I entered once and quickly fled —
I remember now its singing willow rim.

And finally, in that memory all things nurse;
After the city that I finally passed
With scalding unguents spread and smoking darts
The monsoon cut across the delta
At gulf gates . . . There, beyond the dykes

I heard wind flaking sapphire, like this summer,
And willows could not hold more steady sound.

From THE RIVER

All other waters have their time of peace,
Calm, or the turn of tide or summer drought;
But on these bars the tumults never cease,
In violent death this river passes out.

Brimming she goes, a bloody-coloured rush
Hurrying her heaped disorder, rank on rank,
Bubbleless speed so still that in the hush
One hears the mined earth dropping from the bank,

Slipping in little falls whose tingeings drown,
Sunk by the waves for ever pressing on.
Till with a stripping crash the tree goes down,
Its washing branches flounder and are gone.

Then, roaring out aloud, her water spreads,
Making a desolation where her waves
Shriek and give battle, tossing up their heads,
Tearing the shifting sandbanks into graves,

Changing the raddled ruin of her course
So swiftly, that the pilgrim on the shore
Hears the loud whirlpool laughing like a horse
Where the scurfed sand was parched an hour before.

And always underneath that heaving tide
The changing bottom runs, or piles, or quakes
Flinging immense heaps up to wallow wide,
Sucking the surface into whirls like snakes,

If anything should touch that shifting sand,
All the blind bottom sucks it till it sinks;
It takes the clipper ere she comes to land,
It takes the thirsting tiger as he drinks.

And on the river pours – it never tires;
Blind, hungry, screaming, day and night the same
Purposeless hurry of a million ires,
Mad as the wind, as merciless as flame.

From THE NOTEBOOK, NO. 8

The sea – a hammock, a swing, a cradle; it's round
and contained.

But a river – an arrow shot into infinity.

A long road.

The sea – immobility.

A river – motion.

A swimmer's shoulders, a horse's chest splitting
the banks. By moving, the river creates itself.
It doesn't have time to seep into its bed.

MARINA TSVETAEVA (1892–1941)
TRANS. A. MOLOTKOV

SALMON-FISHING

The days shorten, the south blows wide for
    showers now,
The south wind shouts to the rivers,
The rivers open their mouths and the salt salmon
Race up into the freshet.
In Christmas month against the smoulder
    and menace
Of a long angry sundown
Red ash of the dark solstice, you see the anglers,
Pitiful, cruel, primeval,
Like the priests of the people that built Stonehenge,
Dark silent forms, performing
Remote solemnities in the red shallows
Of the river's mouth at the year's turn,
Drawing landward their live bullion, the
    bloody mouths
And scales full of the sunset
Twitch on the rocks, no more to wander at will
The wild Pacific pasture nor wanton and spawning
Race up into fresh water.

THE ESTUARY

Light, stillness and peace lie on the broad sands,
On the salt-marshes the sleep of the afternoon.
The sky's immaculate; the horizon stands
Steadfast, level and clear over the dune.

There are voices of children, musical and thin,
Not far, nor near, there in the sandy hills;
As the light begins to wane, so the tide comes in,
The shallow creek at our feet silently fills:

And silently, like sleep to the weary mind,
Silently, like the evening after the day,
The big ship bears inshore with the inshore wind,
Changes her course, and comes on up through
        the bay,

Rolling along the fair deep channel she knows,
Surging along, right on top of the tide.
I see the flowery wreath of foam at the bows,
The long bright wash streaming away from her side:

I see the flashing gulls that follow her in,
Screaming and tumbling, like children wildly at play,
The sea-born crescent arising, pallid and thin,
The flat safe twilight shore shelving away.

Whether remembered or dreamed, read of or told,
So it has dwelt with me, so it shall dwell with
    me ever:
The brave ship coming home like a lamb to the fold,
Home with the tide into the mighty river.

DELTA

The life that breaks apart in secret streams
I've linked with you:
that argues with itself and almost
seems not to know you, suffocated presence.

When time chokes at its dikes
you rhyme your fate with its immensity,
and surface, memory, more manifest
out of the darkness you descended to,
as now, after rain, green comes back thick
on the branches, crimson cinnabar on the walls.

I know nothing of you but the wordless
message that sustains me on my way:
if you exist as form or a mirage
in the haze of a dream
fed by the shore as it rages, eddies, roars
against the tide.

Nothing of you in the flux of hours,
gray or rent by a flash of sulphur,
other than the whistle of the tugboat
leaving the mist and making for the gulf.

EUGENIO MONTALE (1896–1981)
TRANS. JONATHAN GALASSI

NORTHERN RIVER

When summer days grow harsh
my thoughts return to my river,
fed by white mountain springs,
beloved of the shy bird, the bellbird,
whose cry is like falling water.
O nighted with the green vine,
lit with the rock-lilies,
the river speaks in the silence,
and my heart will also be quiet.

Where your valley grows wide in the plains
they have felled the trees, wild river.
Your course they have checked, and altered
your sweet Alcaic metre.
Not the grey kangaroo, deer-eyed, timorous,
will come to your pools at dawn;
but their tamed and humbled herds
will muddy the watering places.
Passing their roads and cities
you will not escape unsoiled.

But where, grown old and weary,
stagnant among the mangroves,
you hope no longer – there on a sudden
with a shock like joy, beats up
the cold clean pulse of the tide,
the touch of the sea in greeting;

the sea that encompasses
all sorrow and all delight
and holds the memories
of every stream and river.

RIVER INCIDENT

A shell arched under my toes,
Stirred up by a whirl of silt
That riffled around my knees.
Whatever I owed to time
Slowed in my human form;
Sea water stood in my veins,
The elements I kept warm
Crumbled and flowed away,
And I knew I had been there before,
In that cold, granitic slime,
In the dark, in the rolling water.

RIVER

Mother,
Why is the river laughing?
Well, it's because the sun tickles the river.

Mother,
Why is the river singing?
It's because the skylark praised the river's voice.

Mother,
Why is the river cold?
For the memory of having once been loved by
      the snow.

Mother,
How old is the river?
Same age as the young spring, forever.

Mother,
Why doesn't the river rest?
Well, that's because the mother sea
Is waiting for the river to come home.

SHUNTARŌ TANIKAWA (b. 1931)
TRANS. NAOKO ISHIKURA SMITH

AWAITING THE SWIMMER

Light fails, in crossing a river.
The current shines deeply without it.
I hold a white cloth in my hands.
The air turns over one leaf.
One force is left in my arms
To handle the cloth, spread it gently,
And show where I stand above water.

I see her loosed hair straining.
She is trying to come to me, here.
I cannot swim, and she knows it.
Her gaze makes the cloth burn my hands.
I can stand only where I am standing.
Shall she fail, and go down to the sea?
Shall she call, as she changes to water?

She swims to overcome fear.
One force is left in her arms.
How can she come, but in glory?
The current burns; I love
That moving-to-me love, now passing
The midst of the road where she's buried.
Her best motions come from the river;

Her fear flows away to the sea.
The way to move upon water
Is to work lying down, as in love.
The way to wait in a field
Is to hold a white cloth in your hands
And sing with the sound of the river.
Called here by the luminous towel,

My rib-humming breath, and my love,
She steps from the twilit water.
At the level of my throat, she closes
Her eyes, and ends my singing.
I wrap her thin form in the towel,
And we walk through the motionless grasses
To the house, where the chairs we sit in

Have only one force in their arms.
The bed like the river is shining.
Yet what shall I do, when I reach her
Through the moon opened wide on the floor-boards?
What can I perform, to come near her?
How hope to bear up, when she gives me
The fear-killing moves of her body?

JAMES DICKEY (1923–97)   235

WHERE WATER COMES TOGETHER
WITH OTHER WATER

I love creeks and the music they make.
And rills, in glades and meadows, before
they have a chance to become creeks.
I may even love them best of all
for their secrecy. I almost forgot
to say something about the source!
Can anything be more wonderful than a spring?
But the big streams have my heart too.
And the places streams flow into rivers.
The open mouths of rivers where they join the sea.
The places where water comes together
with other water. Those places stand out
in my mind like holy places.
But these coastal rivers!
I love them the way some men love horses
or glamorous women. I have a thing
for this cold swift water.
Just looking at it makes my blood run
and my skin tingle. I could sit
and watch these rivers for hours.
Not one of them like any other.
I'm 45 years old today.
Would anyone believe it if I said
I was once 35?
My heart empty and sere at 35!
Five more years had to pass

before it began to flow again.
I'll take all the time I please this afternoon
before leaving my place alongside this river.
It pleases me, loving rivers.
Loving them all the way back
to their source.
Loving everything that increases me.

RAYMOND CARVER (1938–88)   237

IN A JON BOAT DURING
A FLORIDA DAWN

Sunlight displaces stars
and on the Wakulla
long cypress shadows streak water burning
light and clear. If you look around you,
as you must, you see the bank dividing itself
into lights and darks, black waterbugs
stirring around algae beds, watermarks circling
gray trunks of cypress and oak,
a cypress knee fading under a darker moccasin,
silver tips of river grass breaking
through lighted water, silver backs of mullet
streaking waves of river grass.
For now, there are no real colors, only tones
promising change, a sense
of something developing, and no matter
how many times you have been here,
in this boat or another,
you feel an old surprise surfacing
in and around you. If you could,
you would cut the outboard
and stop it all right here at the gray height
of that anticipation. You would hide yourself
in this moment, cling to an oak branch
or a river snag
and stop even the slightest drift of the current.

In fresh sunlight distinguishing loggerhead
from stump, moss from stone,
you would give yourself completely
to the holding,
like the lizard clinging to the reed cover
or the red tick anchored in the pit of your knee.

RIVER

Something has opened that is neither me
nor you but between,
                   the mouth of the river

opening to sea, and the tide coming in
in a long shining track of sunlight;
                        who do I speak to

but you, neither awake nor asleep
but moving, rolling in, flowing out
                     like breath

and the song that you heave with your slow,
    thick body,

python the colour of wet sand,
                      ongoing, a presence

that walks like a spirit beside us,

                alive

TILLYDRONE MOTTE
Seaton Park, Aberdeen

I played my childhood here on this highest edge,
this hill, in this park: my garden
spread out for me two hundred feet below,
the Don coursing through it, out towards the sea.
Fifteen years in every kind of light and weather:
my castle-keep, watchtower,
anchorite's cell, my solitary
proving ground, a vast sounding board
here amongst the gorse and seabirds.

As the river terraces below me filled with cloud
I stood over it all, making a ghost, a brocken spectre,
trying to cast the shadow of a man.

I knew all the places to disappear, to go
where you couldn't be seen from the path:
the pillbox, the tree house, that secret beach
and hidden above it, the charmed wood. I knew
where the hawthorn tree stands,
bent and fixed like blown smoke,
the sun skimmering in the twist of the river water,
the rough hand of the sea wind in the elms
and sycamores, the soft courtesy of snow.
I knew where to find the cloaked heron,
the cormorant clergy, where I once saw
the swan in the rapids with the Don in spate,

knew the names of the brothers
that drowned there, at the mill turn
– the Crook of Don – where the river tightens in,
where sweetwater meets the brine reaches. I knew
how it came down through the braes and weirs
to the green sluice under the hill, to coast
its way past Walker's Haugh and Kettock's Mill
to the Devil's Rock, drawing
deep through Tam's Hole and the Pot, over
the Black Neuk of the Brig o' Balgownie
where the river rests before the last pull
through the machair and out
to the sea beyond.

A distant smatter of applause and, seconds later,
I see the flock lifting, down in the valley,
losing itself in the far pines.

What I didn't know was this:
that there would come a time when I would find
the trees unclimbable, the river too fast to ford,
that I would learn it wasn't a motte at all
– this place I went to be born –
but a Bronze Age burial cairn,
and not Tillydrone either
– this place where I stood my pale cross –
but *tulach draighionn*, which means,
and has always meant, "the hill of thorns."

SEDIMENT

As dying rivers go, the one they say carries us
like branch-woven baskets into the waiting
hands of a greater current isn't so bad. Those
I remember from childhood tended to steer
our little paper boats sealed with beeswax –
as if that meant waterproof, as if there were no
such thing as sink or swallow – toward storm
drains & the toothy clowns that live in them.
A few years later, after swapping monsters
for whiskey & matches, sex or what rightly
should be called attempts, the rivers seemed
drunk on former glories, like gods returned
to earth to find belief only goes one way.
Have the myths changed that much or simply
our listening? Arroyo. Wash. Dried-out gulch
shaped by eons to fit our burgeoning fires;
the same flame that drove our ancestors west
& begged Odysseus home. Let's follow this
arid crust of clay & scrub as far as its story
takes us. They say there's an ocean out there
somewhere. Eternity & gulls. Undertows. Calm.
A kind of drowning we can learn to breathe.

JOHN SIBLEY WILLIAMS (b. 1978)

SLUICE ANGEL

Low tide at the sea lock,
    a forty foot drop to muddy shallows . . .
        One boat's width

    of channel that the dredger grubs up
        daily . . . Silt to one side scored in circles

        where they dragged for don't ask what . . .

The tall shut doors of the hall
    of the world at which the weight of water,
        of *incipience*, does not need to knock:

    feel it there like a shudder
        of difference, the engine of change.

        Now, almost soundless, hinges shift.

With a gradual calibrated rip
    like a concord of lathes, with a crypt smell,
        two green-grey-brown stiffening blades

    of water fold in. They curve, feathering
        themselves in free fall: wings

        flexed, shuddering, not to soar

but to pour themselves down, to earth
the charge, liquid solid as rock
and untouchable, trouncing itself

to a froth, to exhaustion, till with a sigh
the gates can open, and the world,

our world, small craft, come through.

THE DELTA

If you are going there by foot, prepare
to get wet. You are not you anymore.

You are a girl standing in a pool
of clouds as they catch fire in the distance.

There are laws of heaven and those of place
and those who see the sky in the water,

angels in ashes that are the delta's now.
They say if you sweep the trash from your house

after dark, you sweep away your luck.
If you are going by foot, bring a stick,

a third leg, and honor the great disorder,
the great broom of waterfowl and songbirds.

Prepare to voodoo your way, best you can,
knowing there is a little water in things

you take for granted, a little charity
and squalor for the smallest forms of life.

Voodoo was always mostly charity.
People forget. If you shake a tablecloth

outside at night, someone in your family
dies. There are laws we make thinking

it was us who made them. We are not us.
We are a floodplain by the Mississippi

that once poured slaves upriver to the fields.
We are a hurricane in the making.

We could use a magus who knows something
about suffering, who knows a delta's needs.

We understand if you want a widow
to stay single, cut up her husband's shoes.

He is not himself anyway and walks
barefoot across a landscape that has no north.

Only a ghost tree here and there, a frog,
a cricket, a bird. And if the fates are kind,

a girl with a stick, who is more at home,
being homeless, than you will ever be.

BRUCE BOND (b. 1954)   247

THE HUNGER

You led me to a night hawk
circling orchards for mice,

lantern moon,

diamond eyes
of an 80-year-old sturgeon
cruising the river bank
like a forgotten Indian god.

We walked in the hour
skeleton oaks
reached out of hiding
to touch,

just a short time
before the tide moved in
and this place became
invisible.

ACKNOWLEDGMENTS

Thanks are due to the following copyright holders for permission to reprint:

A. R. AMMONS: "River" from *Collected Poems: 1951–1971*, W. W. Norton & Co. ANON.: from *The Epic of Gilgamesh*, translated by Andrew George, from *The Epic of Gilgamesh*, Penguin, 1999. GUILLAUME APOLLINAIRE: "Mirabeau Bridge". Translation copyright © by Chloe Hughes. Reprinted with permission. W. H. AUDEN: "River Profile", copyright © 1966 by W. H. Auden; from *Collected Poems* by W. H. Auden, edited by Edward Mendelson. Used by permission of Random House, an imprint and division of Penguin Random House LLC. All rights reserved. Copyright © 1966 by W. H. Auden. Reprinted by permission of Curtis Brown, Ltd. All rights reserved. MATSUO BASHO: "Mogami River" and "Hot Summer Day". Translation copyright © by Naoko Ishigura Smith. Reprinted with permission. WENDELL BERRY: "The River Voyagers" (*Poetry Magazine*, Nov. 1959). Reprinted with permission from the poet. JOHN BETJEMAN: "Henley-on-Thames" from *Collected Poems*, John Murray, 1979. BUDDHADĀSA BHIKKHU: "The River Bends but the Water Does Not" (Thai author, 1906–1993). Translation copyright © by Robert A. Troyer and Dylan J. Hartmann and reprinted with permission. ROBERT BLY: "Driving Toward the Lac Qui Parle River" from *Silence in Snowy Fields*, Wesleyan University Press, 1962. PAULA BOHINCE: "La Seine". Copyright © by Paula Bohince. Reprinted with permission from the author. EAVAN BOLAND: "Anna Liffey" from *A Poet's Dublin*, W. W. Norton & Co., 2016. Carcanet Press, Manchester, UK. BRUCE BOND: "The Delta" published in *Poetry Magazine* (July/ Aug. 2013). Reprinted with permission from the author. DAVID BOTTOMS: "In a Jon Boat During a Florida Dawn" from *Armored Hearts: Selected and New Poems*. Copyright © 1995 by David Bottoms. Reprinted with the permission of The Permissions

JAMES DICKEY: "Awaiting the Swimmer" from *Poems, 1957–1967*, Wesleyan University Press, 1967. EMILY DICKINSON: "My River Runs to Thee" and "Least Rivers". Harvard University Press. T. S. ELIOT: Extract from: "The Dry Salvages" from *The Complete Poems and Plays*, Harcourt, Brace & Co., 1952, part of HarperCollins US. Faber & Faber Ltd. Reprinted with permission. LOUISE ERDRICH: "I Was Sleeping Where the Black Oaks Move" from *Original Fire: Selected and New Poems*, HarperCollins, 2003. KIT EVANS: "Riverbed Blues". Reprinted with permission from the author. U. A. FANTHORPE: "Rising Damp" from *Standing To* (1983), and in *Selected Poems* (Penguin, 1999). Enitharmon Editions. ROBERT FROST: "Too Anxious for Rivers" from *The Poetry of Robert Frost*, Henry Holt, 1969. DU FU: "Thoughts on Traveling By Night". Translation copyright © by Jin Lei, reprinted with permission. LOUISE GLÜCK: "Early December in Croton-on-Hudson" from *The First Four Books of Poems*, Ecco Press, HarperCollins, 1995. PHILIP GROSS: "Sluice Angel" from *The Water Table* (Bloodaxe Books, 2009). Reproduced with permission of Bloodaxe Books. JÓNAS HALLGRÍMSSON: "The Sog, Iceland" from *Bard of Iceland* by Dick Ringler © 2002 by the Board of Regents of the University of Wisconsin System. Reprinted by permission of the University of Wisconsin Press. SAM HAMILL: "A Snapshot of Susitna" from *The Book of Elegiac Geography*, Book Store Press, 1978. OSCAR HAMMERSTEIN II: From "Ol' Man River" (*Showboat*, 1927). Rodgers and Hammerstein Organization. JIM HARRISON: "River III" from *Songs of Unreason.* Copyright © 2011 by Jim Harrison. Used with the permission of The Permissions Company, LLC on behalf of Copper Canyon Press, coppercanyonpress.org H. D.: "Leda", originally published in 1919, in *Norton Anthology of American Literature*. Peters Fraser+Dunlop. SEAMUS HEANEY: "Perch" from *Electric Light*, Faber & Faber Ltd. Reprinted with permission. Farrar, Straus & Giroux, 2001. TRINITY HERR: "Topography" reprinted with permission from the author.

251

permission from the author. WILLIAM MEREDITH: "At the Confluence of the Colorado and the Little Colorado" from *New Yorker Magazine* (April 29, 1972). The William Meredith Foundation. Reprinted with permission. KENJI MIYAZAWA: "Along that Frozen Little River". Translation copyright © by Naoko Ishikura Smith. Reprinted with permission from the translator. EUGENIO MONTALE: "Delta" from *Mediterranean*, 1924. Translation by Jonathan Galassi. TONI MORRISON: Excerpt from "The Site of Memory" from *Inventing the Truth: The Art and Craft of Memoir*, Houghton Mifflin, 1995. PAUL MULDOON: "Clonfeacle" and "The Waking Father" from *New Weather*, Faber & Faber Ltd., 1973. Reprinted with permission. PABLO NERUDA: "Amazon", translated by Jaime Marroquín Arredondo. Carmen Balcells Agency. Translation copyright © by Jaime Marroquín Arrodondo. Reprinted with permission. DUANE NIATUM: "Evening Near the Hoko River" from *Native American Songs and Poems*, ed. Brian Swann, Dover Publications, 1996. GABRIEL OKARA: "The Call of the River Nun". Reproduced from Gabriel Okara: *Collected Poems*, edited by Brenda Marie Osbey, by permission of the University of Nebraska Press. Copyright 2016 by the Board of Regents of the University of Nebraska. MARY OLIVER: "At Black River" from *Why I Wake Early*, Beacon Press, 2004. Charlotte Sheedy Literary Agency in conjunction with Salky Literary Management. UEJIMA ONITSURA: "Below the Jumping Sweetfish". Translation copyright © by Naoko Ishigura Smith. Reprinted with permission. ALICE OSWALD: "Birdwatcher" from *Sleepwalk on the Severn*; extract from *Dart*, published by Faber & Faber Ltd. Reprinted with permission. United Agents. GRACE PALEY: "Suddenly There's Poughkeepsie" published in *New Yorker Magazine* (Dec. 16, 2007). Union Literary and Farrar, Straus & Giroux. RUTH PITTER: "The Estuary" from *Sudden Heaven: The Collected Poems of Ruth Pitter*, Kent State University Press, 2018. © by Mark Pitter. SYLVIA PLATH: "Faun" from *The Collected Poems*, Harper & Row, 1981. VASKO POPA: "Great Lord

Danube" from *Complete Poems 1953–1987* by Vasko Popa, Ed: Francis R. Jones, Tr: Anne Pennington and Francis R. Jones, Anvil Press Poetry. Reprinted by kind permission of Carcanet Press, Manchester, UK. MARCEL PROUST: "The Carafes of the Vivonne". Translation copyright © by Kit Andrews. Reprinted with permission. KATHLEEN RAINE: "By the River Eden" from *Selected Poems*, Lindisfarne Press, 1988. JAMES REANEY: "To the Avon River, Above Stratford, Canada" from *To the Avon River, Above Stratford, Canada*, West Meadow Press, 1991. ANNE RIDLER: "River God's Song" originally published in *The New Yorker* (May 8, 1953), taken from *Collected Poems*. Reprinted with permission from Carcanet Press, Manchester, UK. ROBIN ROBERTSON: "Tillydrone Motte" in *American Scholar* (Dec. 7, 2012). THEODORE ROETHKE: "River Incident" from *The Lost Son and Other Poems*, John Lehmann, 1949. EMILY ROSKO: "Flood Plain" From *Weather Inventions* by Emily Rosko, copyright © 2018 Emily Rosko. Reprinted by permission of The University of Akron Press. Unauthorized duplication not permitted. Reprinted with permission from the author. ZHANG RUOXU: "Moonlight on the Spring River". Translation copyright © by Jin Lei, reprinted with permission. KAY RYAN: "The Niagara River" from *The Niagara River*, Grove Press, 2005. FUJIWARA NO SADAYORI: "Winter Dawn, Uji River". Translation copyright © by Naoko Ishikura Smith. Reprinted with permission from the translator. CARL SANDBURG: "Languages" from *Chicago Poems*, 1916. Also published in *The Complete Poems of Carl Sandburg*, Harcourt, 1969. HarperCollins Publishers. OWEN SHEERS: "Liable to Floods" from *Skirred Hill*, Seren Books, 2005. RCW Literary Agency. STEVIE SMITH: "The River God" from *All the Poems of Stevie Smith*, New Directions, 2016, Faber & Faber Ltd. Reprinted with permission. TRACY K. SMITH: "Wade in the Water" from *Wade in the Water*, Graywolf Press, 2018. GARY SNYDER: "The Canyon Wren" and "River in the Valley" from *Axe Handles*, North Point Press, 1983. WILLIAM STAFFORD: "Ask Me" from *Ask Me:*